Target Reading Comprehension Skills

○ TARGET READING SKILLS FOR LIFE SERIES

AGS
PUBLISHING

Circle Pines, Minnesota 55014-1796
800-328-2560
www.agsnet.com

Acknowledgments

Excerpt from "The Treasure of Lemon Brown" by Walter Dean Myers. Reprinted by permission of Miriam Altchuler Literary Agency, on behalf of Walter Dean Myers. Copyright © 1983, by Walter Dean Myers.

"Metaphor" from *A Sky Full of Poems* by Eve Merriam. Copyright © 1964, 1970, 1973 by Eve Merriam. All rights renewed and reserved. Used by permission of Marian Reiner.

"Dreams" from *The Collected Poems of Langston Hughes* by Langston Hughes, copyright © 1994 by The Estate of Langston Hughes. Used by permission of Alfred A. Knopf, a division of Random House, Inc.

Cover Design

Sarah Bennett

Photo and Illustration Credits

Page 6, © Jose Luis Pelaez, Inc./corbisstockmarket; p. 13, Judy King Rieniets; p. 33, © AP/Wide World Photos; p. 35, © Brown Brothers Photographs; pp. 36, 42, 45, 49, 50, 62, 68, 70, 71, Judy King Rieniets; p. 74, © The Granger Collection, New York; pp. 76, 92, © Brown Brothers Photographs; p. 98 (left), © Bettmann/CORBIS; p. 98 (top), © CORBIS; p. 98 (bottom), © Aaron Horowitz/CORBIS; pp. 108, 116, Judy King Rieniets

Publisher's Project Staff

Associate Director, Product Development: Teri Mathews; Editor: Judy Monroe; Development Assistant: Bev Johnson; Design Manager: Nancy Condon; Senior Designer: Daren Hastings; Technical Specialist: Laura Henrichsen; Desktop Production Artist: Peggy Vlahos; Purchasing Agent: Mary Kaye Kuzma; Senior Marketing Manager/Curriculum: Brian Holl

Development and editorial services by Straight Line Editorial Development, Inc.
Art Direction by Sally Brewer Lawrence

© 2003 AGS Publishing
4201 Woodland Road, Circle Pines, MN 55014-1796
800-328-2560
www.agsnet.com

AGS Publishing is a trademark of American Guidance Service, Inc.

Printed in the United States of America

Product Number 93704
ISBN 0-7854-3368-6

A 0 9 8 7 6 5 4 3

CONTENTS

CONTENTS

INTRODUCTION

Welcome!

Reading is like anything else that matters. In order to be good at it, you have to practice. *Target Reading Comprehension Skills* will help you become a better reader.

Here are some of the things you'll learn:

- ■ **Use word attack strategies to figure out new words.** It's easier than you think to tackle new words—even long ones!

- ■ **Use different reading strategies for different kinds of materials.** There are many different kinds of writing—and they should be read in different ways. This book will show you how to choose the right strategy for the job.

- ■ **Use visuals.** A lot of information can be presented without using words, or with very few words. Timelines, graphs, diagrams, and symbols are some ways of doing this. You'll learn how to read and interpret these and other kinds of visuals.

- ■ **Read better by reading more.** You will read about many topics—and some of what you learn may surprise you. The chapters in this book will help you with all the reading tasks you face—from reading in the classroom to reading in real life.

- ■ **Learn more about yourself.** Your ideas are important. This book will help you think about what you read. It will also give you plenty of chances to express your opinions, and tell you why you feel that way.

With practice and a little help from this book, you'll be reading like a pro in no time!

WORD ATTACK TIPS

Most short words are simple to read. When you come to longer words, though, it's easy to get stumped. Here are some tips for figuring out mysterious words:

- ■ **Look for word parts you know.** Is the word made up of a smaller word you know, plus an ending?

- ■ **Look for letter patterns you know.** Knowing a pattern of letters, like the **ain** in **main,** can help you read other words with that pattern. If you can read **main,** you can also read **train, brainy, stained,** and **raining.**

- ■ **Break the word into parts.** Is the word made up of two smaller words that have been put together?

- ■ **Look for syllables.** The vowels in a word are a clue to how many syllables it has.

- ■ **Look at the letters in the word.** What sounds do the letters stand for? Blend all the sounds together to read the word.

READING STRATEGY TIPS

A strategy is a smart plan for getting a job done. Reading strategies help with the job of reading. Here are some strategies you'll learn to use:

- **Preview and predict.** Looking ahead at a passage can help you know what to expect from it.

- **Set a purpose.** Every time you read, you do it for a reason. Knowing what that reason is can help you understand the text.

- **Think critically.** Reading without thinking is like chewing without swallowing. What's the point? This book will show you how to think about what you read by asking yourself questions.

- **Make the facts stick.** How can you remember what you read? This book will teach you four "memory tricks."

Introduction

What if you came to this word in a book you were reading?

> antiestablishment

Just looking at this word could make your head hurt! But a few simple tricks can help you attack this word and figure it out. You can attack any word, no matter how long it is or how hard it looks. Here are a few things you can do to get the better of a big word.

Divide and Conquer

Break a word into parts. Try it. Draw a line between the fourth and fifth letters.

a n t i e s t a b l i s h m e n t

What word part starts the word?_____

Anti means "against." So the whole word probably means "against something." But against what?

Use Letter Sounds

Try to read the word that is left. It looks long, but it is made up of letters and sounds you know. Try reading it, one part at a time.

es   tab   lish   ment

Blend all the parts together. Does that sound like a word you've heard before?

Think About Meaning

The word **establishment** can mean "the way things are in a society." It refers to what people believe and what the rules are. To be "anti" establishment probably means what?

____ under the city streets
____ against the rules of society
____ badly dressed in public

Good job! You successfully attacked a monster word. In Chapter 1 you will learn more about these and other word attack skills.

LESSON 1   Divide and Conquer

Words Within Words

Even if a word looks new, you may know part of it.

Look at the words below. Try to find a smaller word inside each one.

unworkable	partial	wordiness

1. What smaller word can you find in each word? Check it.

unworkable	**partial**	**wordiness**
___ table	___ part	___ order
___ uncle	___ pants	___ word
___ work	___ tin	___ mess

Use the word parts to help you figure out what each word might mean. Fill in the correct circle below.

2. Partial most likely means_____.

    Ⓐ old pants   Ⓑ tin can   Ⓒ part of

3. Unworkable most likely answers what?

    Ⓐ Will it work?   Ⓑ Is it windy?   Ⓒ Where are you?

4. Wordiness most likely has to do with _____.

    Ⓐ animals   Ⓑ trees   Ⓒ words

VOCABULARY BUILDER

Words come in different forms.

reword
word
wordy   wordiness

Knowing one form can help you figure out other forms.

Letter Patterns

Read these sets of words. Circle the pattern that is the same in each set. One has been done for you.

	5.	**6.**
ch(ange)	little	picture
gr(ange)	kettle	denture
m(ange)r	whittle	fixture
7._____	8. _____	9. _____

Which word below has the same pattern of letters as each group of words above? Write the words where they belong.

mange	throttle	lecture

LESSON 2   Use Letter Sounds

Just a Code

Words are made up of letters. Letters stand for sounds. Written language is like a **code**. With practice, you can break the code.

Consonants

You may never have seen this word before, but you can probably figure out how to say it using letter sounds.

deft

1. Which word below rhymes with this word?

___ deal   ___ deep   ___ left   ___ duct

The word **deft** means "quick or skilled." It ends with two consonant sounds that come together—**f** and **t**.

- Consonants that come together can stand for one sound, two sounds, or three sounds.
- Some consonants are silent.

On the left are some words you may know. On the right are some words you may not know. You can figure out how to say them by sounding them out.

Draw a line from each word on the left to the word that rhymes with it.

2. high	impound
3. around	pall
4. small	bout
5. out	nigh

Find a word from the box that rhymes with each pair of words below. Write it on the line.

clout	sigh	install	resound

6. around, impound, _____   **8.** high, nigh, _____

7. small, pall, _____   **9.** out, bout, _____

Short Vowels and Long Vowels

It's important to think about **vowels** when you try to sound out a word. These letters are the vowels.

a	e	i	o	u

(and sometimes **y**)

Every vowel can have a long sound or a short sound.

Read these words.

Long Vowel Sounds	Short Vowel Sounds
pine	pin
cape	cap
teen	ten
hope	hop
cute	cut

- Words with the consonant-vowel-consonant, or CVC, pattern often have a short vowel sound.
- Words with the consonant-vowel-consonant-*e*, or CVC*e*, pattern often have a long vowel sound.
- Most words with the long **e** sound do not have the CVC*e* pattern— most long **e** words are spelled **ee** or **ea**.

Read these words. Write each word in the chart where it belongs.

tape	mix	beat	sled
fox	bone	slack	
tune	shut	time	

Long Vowels	Short Vowels
10. _____	15. _____
11. _____	16. _____
12. _____	17. _____
13. _____	18. _____
14. _____	19. _____

Attacking Longer Words

Read these longer words and listen to the vowel sound in each part. Then write each word in the correct list.

pinecones	tenspeed	magnet
subject	keepsake	pinstripe

These words have two long vowel sounds.

20. _____ **21.** _____

These words have one long vowel sound and one short vowel sound.

22. _____ **23.** _____

These words have two short vowel sounds.

24. _____ **25.** _____

Reading Words with Endings

Many words have endings like **ed** and **ing** added to them. How do you know if the vowel sound in the first part of the word is long or short?

Read these words.

> hope + ing = hoping
> hop + ing = hopping

26. What letter was dropped from **hope**? _____

27. What letter was added to **hop**? _____

The new words, **hoping** and **hopping**, may look different than they did before the endings were added. But the vowel sound in the first part of each word is the same.

Write a word from the box to complete each sentence.

tapping	scrapped
taping	scraped

28. Rex is _____ the sides of the box shut.

29. I think that _____ sound is being made by a woodpecker.

30. I _____ the scales from the fish.

31. Lisa _____ her plan for a dog-walking club.

SPELLING BUILDER

When you add **ed** or **ing** to a word that ends in silent **e**, drop the **e**.

If you're adding these endings to a CVC word with a short vowel sound, double the last consonant.

More Long Vowels

Vowels can be tricky. That's because different letter patterns can stand for the same vowel sound.

Read these words. Draw a line under all the letters in bold type.

Long *a*	Long *e*	Long *i*	Long *o*	Long *u*
cape	teen	pine	hope	cute
tail	team	high	know	new
bay	we	try	boat	too

Now finish these rhymes. Write each word in the box on a line. Use the letter patterns above to help you.

quail	foal	newt	loam

32. a cute _____

33. a _____ with a goal

34. a _____ in a tale

35. some _____ by your home

Read each word in bold type. Put a check next to the word that rhymes with it.

36. mail ___ mall ___ tale ___ mate

37. beet ___ stem ___ teen ___ treat

38. two ___ grew ___ twin ___ tow

39. sigh ___ sick ___ fly ___ strike

40. boat ___ tote ___ bat ___ bone

41. foam ___ for ___ fame ___ dome

42. flute ___ flux ___ boot ___ flue

Just for Fun

Try to say the name of this Hawaiian fish.

humuhumu-nukunuku-a-pua'a*

*also called a triggerfish

LESSON 3   Using Related Words

All in the Family

A **word family** is a group of words that look alike and have related meanings. Knowing one word in the family can help you read related words.

Read each word in bold type and think about its meaning. Then put a check next to four other words in the same family.

1. **safe**   ___ safety   ___ sandwich   ___ safekeeping

            ___ sofa   ___ safely   ___ safeguard

2. **pass**   ___ impasse   ___ pants   ___ patted

            ___ passage   ___ passerby   ___ passable

WRITING TIP

If you know word families, you will have more than one way to express an idea when you write. Vary your writing by using related words.

Who Isn't Related?

Cross out the word in each list that does not belong to the word family.

3. writer, write, wreak, written

4. changing, chanting, change, exchange

5. deep, depend, deeply, deepness

6. sleepy, sleepless, sledding, asleep

Write a word from the box to complete each sentence. The words after each sentence tell you the word family of the missing word.

passage	sleepless	deepness
written	exchange	safekeeping

7. I will put your ring in this box for _____. (related to **safe**)

8. We found a _____ through the maze. (related to **pass**)

9. This sentence must have been _____ by a little kid! (related to **write**)

10. The _____ of the lake shocked me. (related to **deep**)

11. Tim needs to _____ his new pants for a different size. (related to **change**)

12. After two _____ nights, Janelle was a wreck. (related to **sleep**)

Words That Share the Same Root

Many English words come from the ancient language of Greek or Latin. Knowing the meaning of some Greek and Latin roots can help you figure out many words that look new.

The Latin root **act** comes from a word that means "do." This web shows some words that have this root.

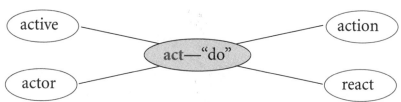

13. Which word below probably shares the Latin root **act**?

   Ⓐ art   Ⓒ fact

   Ⓑ enact   Ⓓ ant

The Greek root **cycl** comes from a word that means "ring or circle." This web shows some words that have this root.

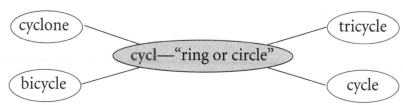

14. Which word below probably shares the Greek root **cycl**?

   Ⓐ clam   Ⓒ city

   Ⓑ recycle   Ⓓ car

15. A **cyclone** is a kind of storm. How do you think a **cyclone** moves? (Hint: Look at the meaning of the root word **cycl**.)

   Ⓐ from up to down   Ⓒ in a circle

   Ⓑ in a line   Ⓓ from east to west

16. The Latin root **uni** means "one." What does the word **unite** probably mean?

   Ⓐ one night long ago   Ⓒ twist into a circle

   Ⓑ look-alikes   Ⓓ join together into one

17. What is a **unicycle**? (Hint: Think about the meaning of the roots **uni** and **cycle**.)

   Ⓐ one storm   Ⓒ a clam with one shell

   Ⓑ a bike with one wheel   Ⓓ all that exists

LESSON 4   Finding the Base Word

Think Small

A **base word** is the main building block of a word. Many longer words are made up of one short word plus word parts added to the beginning or the end.

Read these words. Circle the base word in each one. Write that word on the line. An example has been done for you.

Example		
	re(call)ing	call

1. disarmed _____

3. unworldly _____

2. pretreated _____

4. longingly _____

Base Words Can Change

Sometimes a base word changes when an ending is added.

Read the words below and answer the questions.

5. **changing**   What letter was dropped from **change** when the **ing** ending was added? _____

6. **stopping**   What letter was added to **stop** when the **ing** ending was added? _____

7. **silliness**   What letter in **silly** changed to **i** when the **ness** ending was added? _____

8. **supplies**   What letter in **supply** changed to **i** when the **es** ending was added? _____

Find the Base Word

Read each word in bold type. Put a check next to the base word.

9. **renumbering** ___ boring ___ remember ___ number ___ ringing

10. **unlimited** ___ mites ___ limit ___ unlined ___ limp

11. **remaking** ___ king ___ make ___ making ___ remake

12. **pretest** ___ test ___ pretty ___ rested ___ retest

Prefixes and Suffixes

A **prefix** is a word part that can be added to the beginning of a word. Here are some prefixes and their meanings.

prefix	meaning	example	meaning
un	"not"	undone	"not done"
pre	"before"	premake	"make before"
re	"again"	rewrap	"wrap again"

A **suffix** is a word part added to the end of a word. Here are some suffixes and their meanings.

suffix	meaning	example	meaning
ly	"in a way that is"	quickly	"in a quick way"
less	"without"	hatless	"without a hat"
able	"able to be done"	lovable	"able to be loved"

Write each word in the box in the sentence where it belongs. Use the meaning of the prefix, suffix, and base word.

premade	lovable
hatless	rewrap

13. Todd bought sandwiches that had been made earlier. Todd bought _____ sandwiches.

14. Beline went out in the wind with no hat on. Beline was _____.

15. These are people you could become fond of. The people are _____.

16. Rip the paper off that gift and try again. You must _____ it.

Write a word from the box to finish each sentence.

unthinkable	civilized	painstakingly	whimsical

17. Mom said, "_____ people do not eat peas with their hands."

18. It is _____ that my cat and my dog will ever like each other.

19. A whim is a quick, funny idea that jumps into your brain. Which word most likely tells about such an idea? _____

20. If you took pains to do something just so, how did you do it?

_____

Reading Compound Words

Two Words into One

A **compound word** is made from two smaller words. You can often figure out what a compound word means by thinking about what the smaller words mean.

Write the two smaller words inside each compound word below.

Example		
outside	out	+ side

1. another _____ + _____

2. cutout _____ + _____

3. airbag _____ + _____

Write each compound word from the box next to its meaning.

landform	greenhouse	newcomer

4. a hill, valley, or bluff _____

5. warm place where plants grow indoors_____

6. one who has just come to a place _____

Longer Compound Words

The words below are made up of a compound word plus a prefix or ending.

Read each word. Then write all the word parts that make it up.

Example			
relandscape =	re	+ land	+ scape

7. carpooling = _____ + _____ + _____

8. skateboarding = _____ + _____ + _____

9. undoable = _____ + _____ + _____

LESSON 6 Syllables

How Many Syllables?

A word can have one or more syllables. A syllable has at least one vowel.

Circle the vowels in the words below.

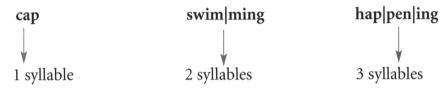

cap	**swim|ming**	**hap|pen|ing**
↓	↓	↓
1 syllable	2 syllables	3 syllables

Circle each vowel in the words below. Then write those words in the chart below where they belong.

1. establish   **2.** magnet   **3.** brim

1 syllable	2 syllables	3 syllables
4. _____	**5.** _____	**6.** _____

A syllable can have more than one vowel letter.

Read the words below. Circle the vowel or vowels in each syllable.

> **Examples**
>
> roadblock   sailboat

7. entering   **8.** mainstream   **9.** pumping   **10.** painstaking

Notice that two vowels in a syllable work together to make one vowel sound.

Dividing Between Consonants

Many words are divided into syllables in between the consonants, like this:

   brim\|ming   mag\|net   can\|non\|ball

Divide the words below into syllables. Draw a line in between each pair of consonants. Then, write how many syllables each word has.

11. establish _____   **13.** summer _____

12. sailboat _____   **14.** tamper_____

> **READING TIP**
>
> When two or more consonants stand for the same sound, the consonants stay together when the word is divided into syllables.
>
> ling\|er   pack\|ing
>
> wish\|ing   match\|less

Long Vowel or Short Vowel?

Read these words. Write L next to each word with a long vowel sound. Write S next to each word with a short vowel sound.

15. he _____

16. I _____

17. no _____

18. it _____

19. on _____

20. met _____

21. Do the words that have a long vowel sound end with a consonant or a vowel?
___ consonant   ___ vowel

22. Do the words that have a short vowel sound end with a consonant or a vowel?
___ consonant   ___ vowel

Examples

A syllable that ends with a consonant usually has a short vowel sound.   it   met

A syllable that ends with a vowel usually has a long vowel sound.   he   no

---

Some words have only one consonant in between the syllables.

comet	pilot

Is the vowel sound in the first syllable of **comet** long or short? Is the vowel sound in the first syllable of **pilot** long or short? To answer these questions, think about what kind of letter the syllable ends with. (If it ends with a vowel, the vowel is long. If it ends with a consonant, the vowel is short.)

Examples

com|et   pi|lot   plan|et   mo|tor

Try It Out

Read each word in the box aloud. Draw a line to divide it into syllables. Then write each word in the sentence where it belongs.

comics	tuna	razor	topic

23. Deke made _____ fish sandwiches for lunch.

24. My dad shaves with a _____.

25. Liza likes to read the _____, but not the rest of the news.

26. What is the _____ of your paper?

LESSON 7   Using Context Clues

Weird Words and How to Read Them

Some words are easy to read using letter sounds, but their meanings may be unclear.

Read these words.

whangee	sigmoid	papule

What in the world do these words mean? There are no good clues inside these words to help you figure that out. But there is hope! Often you can use the other words in a sentence to help you figure out the meaning of a weird word. Using other words in a sentence to help you figure out the meaning of a new word is called using **context clues**.

Read these sentences. Fill in the circle beside the most likely meaning of the word in bold type. Then underline the context clues in each sentence that helped you figure out the meaning of whangee, sigmoid, **and** papule.

THINK ABOUT IT

When you come to an unknown word, ask yourself, "What other word would make sense here?"

1. Stuart made a walking stick out of the thick stem of a **whangee** plant. A **whangee** is probably a _____.

   Ⓐ new sneaker

   Ⓑ kind of bug

   Ⓒ long trip through the grass

   Ⓓ kind of tree or shrub

2. That snake has a **sigmoid** shape—it looks like a big green S! **Sigmoid** probably means _____.

   Ⓐ snake-like

   Ⓑ green

   Ⓒ having an s-shape

   Ⓓ making a hissing sound

3. Angela hoped that her make-up would hide the big red **papule** on her chin. A **papule** is probably _____.

   Ⓐ a big red bug

   Ⓑ another word for face

   Ⓒ anything that could make you feel funny

   Ⓓ another word for pimple

More Weird Words

Read the sentences below. Use context clues to help you figure out the meaning of the words in bold type. Fill in the correct circle.

4. Rex left the door **ajar,** and a cold wind blew into the house. **Ajar** probably means _____.

    Ⓐ in a house   Ⓒ a little bit open

    Ⓑ not hot or cold   Ⓓ one jar

5. Mrs. Beek said never to use an **ampersand** in place of the word **and.** An **ampersand** is probably this mark:

    Ⓐ &   Ⓒ ?

    Ⓑ :   Ⓓ @

6. The **whelks** we found in the sea looked just like the snails you see on land. **Whelks** are probably _____.

    Ⓐ sailors   Ⓒ animal tracks

    Ⓑ sea snails   Ⓓ big fish

7. The mouse was too **trepid** to step out of its hole. **Trepid** probably means _____.

    Ⓐ very, very shy   Ⓒ having an s-shape

    Ⓑ very, very small   Ⓓ overfed

8. The pain in Jeff's leg was so **acute** that he yelled every time he moved it. **Acute** probably means _____.

    Ⓐ very cute   Ⓒ very soft

    Ⓑ very bad   Ⓓ very red

Words with More Than One Meaning

Let's say you come to the word **trunk** when you are reading. **Trunk** can mean the back part of a car, a place for keeping old clothes, or an elephant's nose. How do you know which meaning is being used? Look for context clues.

Read these sentences. Use context clues to figure out the meaning of each word in bold type. Then put a check beside the correct meaning.

9. "I do not have enough cash to pay this **bill**," Gina said.

___ bird beak

___ money owed

10. It was so hot inside Dad turned on the **fan**.

___ machine that cools a room

___ person who likes a rock star

11. Hit the ball with the **bat** as hard as you can.

___ stick used in baseball

___ little flying animal

12. You should **sand** that desk before you paint it.

___ little bits of rock

___ to rub with sandpaper

13. I keep water, a flashlight, and a radio in my **trunk**.

___ back part of a car

___ elephant's nose

14. I need to **trim** the branches away from the window.

___ cut back

___ thin and fit

Using Context and Word Roots

You can use context and word roots to figure out a word's meaning.

Read these sentences. Then answer the questions.

On the day of the big bike race, the road was full of **cyclists**.

15. The root of **cyclists** is _____.

Ⓐ **cyclone,** meaning "spinning storm"

Ⓑ **ice cream**

Ⓒ **bi,** meaning "two"

Ⓓ **cycl,** meaning "circle or ring"

16. In this sentence, **cyclists** are riding _____.

Ⓐ bicycles

Ⓑ unicycles

Ⓒ tricycles

Ⓓ ponies

LESSON 8   Looking It Up

Why Use a Dictionary?

Let's say you are making a cake with a friend. The recipe tells you to decorate the top of the cake with "a ring of **nonpareils**." Your friend thinks **nonpareils** is another word for **parachute**. You think it means "two lines side-by-side." Neither meaning makes sense. What can you do? You can look up that weird word in a dictionary.

A **dictionary** is a book that lists most or all of the words in a language, in ABC order. A dictionary tells you four things:
- how to say a word
- what the word means
- how the word is used
- where the word came from

A dictionary entry for **nonpareil** might look like this:

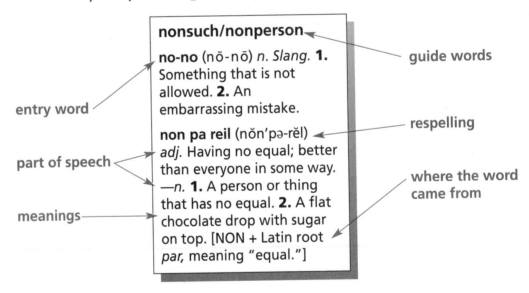

guide words

entry word

part of speech

meanings

respelling

where the word came from

Use the dictionary entry to answer these questions.

1. The sign **n.** stands for **noun**. (A noun is a word that names a person, place, or thing.) How many meanings does **nonpareil** have when it is used as a noun?

   Ⓐ one

   Ⓑ two

   Ⓒ three

   Ⓓ four

2. Read the noun meanings for **nonpareil**. Which meaning do you think the cookbook is using? Write it here.

_____

3. The entry word shows how **nonpareil** is split into syllables. How many syllables does it have?

(A) one   (C) three

(B) two   (D) four

4. What root does the second part of **nonpareil** come from?

(A) the Latin root **parachute**   (C) the Latin root **par**

(B) the Greek root **part**   (D) the Greek root **party**

5. Look at the entry for **no-no**. How many meanings are given for this word?

(A) one   (C) three

(B) two   (D) four

6. Read this sentence:

Standing on your head at the dinner table is a **no-no**.

What meaning is being used here? Write it on the line.

_____

Try It Out

Read these sentences. Find each word in bold type in a dictionary. Write its meaning on the line. (Remember—use context clues to figure out which meaning is being used!)

Duane was **nattily** dressed for the **recital**.

Mr. Ping is at the **zenith** of his musical **career**.

7. nattily _____

8. zenith _____

9. recital _____

10. career _____

Part A Letters and Sounds

- You can figure out many new words by sounding them out.
- Think about the sounds the letters stand for.
- Look for letter patterns you know, such as **igh** and **able**.
- Think about letter patterns that often stand for vowel sounds, such as the CVCe pattern in **tame** and the CVC pattern in **tam**.

On the left are some words you may know. On the right are some words you may not have seen before. You can figure out how to say them by using letter sounds. Draw a line from each word on the left to the word on the right that rhymes with it.

1. night   resound
2. bucked   slumber
3. number   blight
4. form   duct
5. around   norm

Write a word from the box to complete each sentence.

hopping	hoping	ridding	riding

6. Gwen is _____ to see some animals on her trip.
7. I spotted a rabbit _____ along the path.
8. I am _____ my life of stress.
9. Was that Daniel _____ in the red car?

Part B Divide and Conquer

- You can read many longer words by dividing them into smaller parts.
- Look for the base word.
- Look for a prefix at the beginning of a base word or an ending at the end.
- Try splitting words into syllables.

Put a check mark next to the base word of each word in bold type

1. deformed
___ foam
___ form
___ formal

2. unchanging
___ change
___ uncle
___ chaining

3. revisited
___ revved
___ sites
___ visit

Write the prefix, base word, and ending in each word.

4. deformed   _____ + _____ + _____
5. unchanging _____ + _____ + _____
6. revisited   _____ + _____ + _____

Write each word next to its meaning.

deformed	unchanging	revisited

7. went back to see again_____

8. always the same_____

9. made in the wrong shape _____

Write the number of syllables in each word on the line.

10. sleeplessness _____

11. magnet _____

12. avidly _____

13. allotment _____

14. slight _____

15. timing _____

Write each word in the sentence where it belongs. Use the meaning of the base word and the prefix or suffix.

resend	unworkable	clueless
partly	preheat	unjustly

16. Before you put the cake in, _____ the oven to 400°.

17. A plan to start a farm on Mars would be _____.

18. You must _____ that letter, and this time please put a stamp on it.

19. Gus is only _____ through with his lunch.

20. To be _____ is to not know a thing.

21. Tad was _____ blamed for the mess.

Write a compound word from the box to complete each sentence.

pancakes	throughout	underwater
soundstage	yearbook	

22. Please write your name in the _____ under your picture.

23. Part of the film was shot on a _____.

24. Jen got an _____ camera for diving.

25. It is hot in the tropics _____ the year.

26. I like to put blueberries on my _____.

Part C

Think About Meaning

■ Use context clues, related words, and root words to help you figure out the meanings of new words.

■ For words with more than one meaning, use context clues to help you figure out which meaning is being used.

Read each word in bold type and think about its meaning. Then put a check next to the two other words that are in the same family.

1. **form**　　___ transform　　___ reform　　___ fort

2. **rate**　　___ unrated　　___ ratted　　___ rating

3. **please**　　___ pleasing　　___ pleasant　　___ plaster

Use context clues to figure out the meaning of each word in bold type. Then fill in the correct circle.

4. A bright **beacon** shines on the cliff to show ships where the rocks are.

　Ⓐ meat that goes with eggs　　Ⓒ a light or signal

　Ⓑ what a bird pecks with　　Ⓓ a good deed

5. We pinned a **nosegay** made of roses to the speaker's jacket so people would know who she was.

　Ⓐ a small bunch of flowers　　Ⓒ a nametag

　Ⓑ a glass of water　　Ⓓ a happy nose

6. The king's men **quashed** the revolt and sent the rebels back to their homes in defeat.

　Ⓐ drank　　Ⓒ let in

　Ⓑ put down by force　　Ⓓ became part of

7. The old homes were **razed** and new ones were put in their place.

　Ⓐ fixed up for sale　　Ⓒ wrecked or torn down

　Ⓑ shaved with a blade　　Ⓓ kidded or teased

Use context clues to figure out the meaning of the word in bold type. Then put a check beside the correct meaning.

8. "Sit down for a **spell** and rest your legs," Grandma said.

　___ write the letters in a word　　___ short time

9. I do not know where that jet will **land.**

　___ what we walk on　　___ set down

Advanced Word Attack/Looking It Up

Part D

Read each sentence below. Then answer the questions.

> The cold lands near the top of the world
> are mostly **unpeopled**.

The word **unpeopled**…

1. is related to: _____

   Ⓐ poppy   Ⓑ peony   Ⓒ people

2. has these word parts:

   _____ + _____ + _____

3. probably means _____.

   Ⓐ full of people   Ⓒ unlike poppies

   Ⓑ without any people   Ⓓ peony-like

> I saw a big ox **lumber** over the hill toward the pond.

The word **lumber**…

4. rhymes with: _____

   Ⓐ number   Ⓑ limber   Ⓒ lump

5. probably means _____ in the sentence above.

   Ⓐ trees cut for wood   Ⓒ move fast

   Ⓑ sleep soundly   Ⓓ move in a clumsy way

6. Look up **lumber** in a dictionary. What guide words do you see at the top of the page? _____ and _____

7. How many entries are given for **lumber**? _____

8. What is a meaning for **lumber** other than the one used in the sentence above?

   _____

Introduction

Figuring out words is just one part of being a good reader. Good readers also **think about** the act of reading. They ask themselves questions like these:

- What kind of book or story is this?
- What do I already know about books or stories like this?
- What will this book or story probably be like, based on what I know?
- Will I read this just for fun, or will I read it to learn facts I'll need to remember?

Good readers think about what they read—**before** reading, **while** reading, and **after** reading. They use strategies that help them to understand and remember what they read.

What Is a Strategy?

A **strategy** is a plan. You may not know it, but you use strategies every day. Strategies are useful for all kinds of real-life tasks.

Read each task description on the left. Then draw a line to match each task with a logical first step for getting it done.

The task is...	Do this first...
It's your job to do a monster pile of dishes.	Make a shopping list.
You have to cook hot dogs for 75 people.	Find rubber gloves, soap, and towels.
You want to win a football game, and you want it bad!	Practice hard and work as a team.

Great job! You just used **strategic thinking**.

Now pick one task from above. On the lines below, tell how you would get it done. Use strategic thinking to plan out the steps.

My strategy for _____ :

_____

_____

In Chapter 2 you will learn more about strategic reading skills.

READING TIP

Think about the things you do while you read. Which things help you read better? Which things get in the way?

Strategies for Reading

Vocabulary for Reading Strategies

These words are important when you talk about reading strategies.

Read the words and their meanings.

fic|tion	a story made up by a writer and often read just for fun
non|fic|tion	any written work that tells about a real person, place, or thing
pur|pose	a reason for doing something—in this case, your reason for reading
pre|dic|tion	a smart guess about what might happen
ad|just	change
rate	speed
clar|if|y	clear up confusion
cap|tion	a sentence that tells what a photo shows

Read the clues. Then write each word in the puzzle.

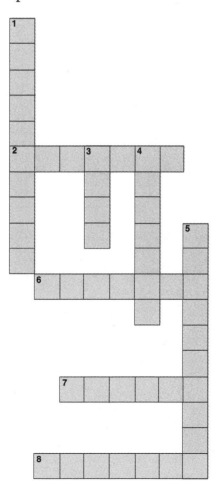

Across

2. If you don't understand something, stop to do this.

6. This means "why you do something."

7. If your seat belt is too tight, _____ it.

8. The _____ explains the picture.

Down

1. This kind of writing tells about real people and events.

3. Use this word to talk about how fast something happens.

4. A story about talking rabbits must be _____.

5. "I think it will rain" is a _____.

LESSON 10   Previewing and Predicting

Before You Read

Before reading a fiction or nonfiction story, **preview** it. To preview is to look at a piece of writing to see what it's about. Here's how:

- Read the title and headings.
- Read the first paragraph.
- Look at any pictures and read the captions.
- Read the Key Words or Words to Know, if any are listed.

After you preview, make a **prediction**—a guess about what might happen in the story. With nonfiction, a prediction often involves predicting what information might be presented.

To preview the article on page 33, follow the steps below.

1. Underline the title. Circle the two headings in bold type. Read the caption and put an X by it.

2. Read the first paragraph. What will this article be about?

   _____

3. Is this article fiction or nonfiction? ___ nonfiction ___ fiction

4. What do you think happened to the tank of molasses?

   _____

   _____

5. How do you think Boston was affected by the disaster?

   _____

   _____

Now read the article on page 33. As you read, find out if your predictions were right.

READING TIP

Nonfiction usually has headings, subheadings, photos, and captions. Fiction stories usually have just text and art.

The Boston Molasses Disaster of 1919

WORDS TO KNOW

molasses

million

flood

elevated

How It Began On January 15, 1919, molasses turned deadly. It was a winter day in Boston that had turned suddenly warm. Near the harbor stood a big tank. It was 58 feet high and 90 feet wide. The tank was almost full of sweet, sticky, brown molasses.

People nearby had stopped working to have lunch. Everyone was talking about the odd heat spell. They did not know that inside the tank, the molasses was heating up too fast.

All of a sudden, the big tank began rumbling. The ground started to shake. Loud popping sounds cut through quiet afternoon as steel bolts snapped. Then the tank exploded! A wall of dark, foaming molasses, 8 feet high, roared out of the tank. The sticky flood swallowed up everything in its path.

Death and Destruction About 2.3 million gallons of molasses rushed out at 35 miles per hour. The oozing flood tossed train cars into the air. It knocked over buildings. It sucked men, women, children, and horses under its deadly grip. An elevated train sped by just as the wave hit. The steel legs holding up the tracks bent and then snapped. The tracks went down. In all, 21 people lost their lives. Over 150 got hurt.

The wave slowed and spread out. Soon many blocks of downtown Boston were covered in brown goo. It took weeks to clean up the mess, but the smell did not go away. For 30 years, a strong smell of molasses hung in the air on hot summer days. Some people say they can still smell molasses when the air heats up.

The streets of Boston were covered in two to three feet of sticky molasses.

After You Read

Finish these sentences:

6. I predicted that _____

_____

_____

7. What really happened was _____

_____

_____

STRATEGY BUILDER

This passage is an example of **narrative nonfiction**. Knowing what nonfiction narrative is like will help you know what to expect the next time you see this kind of writing.

LESSON 11 Setting a Good Purpose

Before You Read

When you **set a purpose** for reading, you decide why you are reading. The purpose you set depends partly on what you are reading.

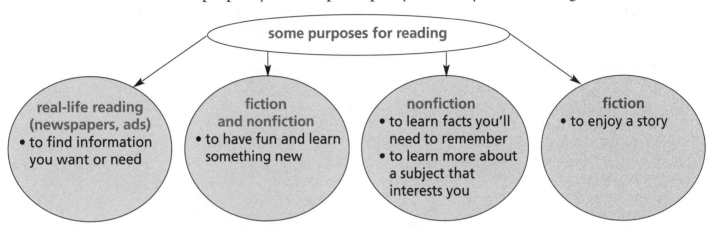

To set a purpose for the passage on page 35, start by previewing it.

1. What is the title of the passage?

_____

2. What does the photograph show?

_____

3. Read the first paragraph. Is the passage fiction or nonfiction?

_____

4. What will be your purpose for reading it? Fill in the correct circle.

   Ⓐ to learn about Bucktown, Maryland

   Ⓑ to learn about a real person, Harriet Tubman

   Ⓒ to find out where the Underground Railroad ended

   Ⓓ to enjoy a fiction story about life long ago

Now read the passage.

Harriet Tubman

WORDS TO KNOW

famous

conductor

overseer

field

The Road to Freedom She was known as "Moses" to slaves who wished to escape into freedom. She was born into slavery, but went on to escape and help many others escape. Their route to freedom was called the "Underground Railroad." Harriet Tubman was its most famous "conductor."

Early Life Harriet Tubman was born in about 1820 in Bucktown, Maryland. At first she worked as a house servant. At about age 12 she was sent to do field work. One day, an angry overseer threatened to strike another field worker. Harriet stood up to block his path. The overseer threw a heavy object, and it hit Harriet by mistake. She fell to the ground. Harriet never fully got over the blow. She had blackouts and sleeping spells from time to time for the rest of her life.

Harriet Tubman was born in 1820 and died in 1913.

A Leader to Her People In 1849 Harriet escaped to Pennsylvania, a free state. In 1851 she snuck back into Maryland and helped her sister and her sister's children escape. In the years that followed she went back to the South about 18 times. All together, she helped close to 300 people travel North to freedom. In 1857, she led her parents to Auburn, New York.

A Network of Courage and Kindness The Underground Railroad was not really a railroad. It was a network of people and safe houses. The people, both black and white, helped escaping slaves find their way over land, rivers, and mountains. Safe houses were homes where kind people fed the fugitives and gave them a place to sleep.

A trip to the North on foot could take weeks or months. The trip was long, hard, and dangerous. Still, many hundreds of slaves made this trip, hoping for freedom in the North.

After You Read

5. Was your purpose for reading met? ___ yes ___ no

6. Who was Harriet Tubman?

_____

_____

_____

7. What important thing did Harriet Tubman do?

_____

_____

_____

Before You Read

Set your own purpose for reading the next passage. First, preview it. Then write your purpose for reading on the lines below.

8. My purpose for reading: _____

Now read the passage.

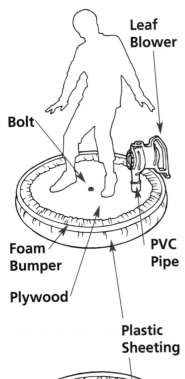

Bolt

Leaf Blower

Foam Bumper

Plywood

PVC Pipe

Plastic Sheeting

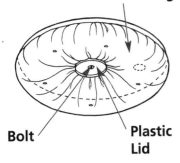

Bolt

Plastic Lid

BOTTOM VIEW

Hoverboards

Riding on Air A hoverboard looks like a scooter, but has no wheels. Unlike a scooter, a hoverboard does not touch the ground. You may be surprised to know that a hoverboard is a simple machine.

How It Works A hoverboard has a board or platform to stand on. It has a machine, such as leaf blower, that fits on top of the board. The machine blows air down through a hole in the board. The board has a skirt of heavy plastic or other material. This hangs to the ground around the sides of the board. When the blower is on, moving air gets trapped under the board. The air rushes around in a circle. Because it cannot escape, the moving air lifts the board off the ground.

Riding a Hoverboard Steering and stopping a hoverboard can be tricky. Going slow often works better than going fast. Homemade hoverboards can be steered by leaning left or right. Because falls can be dangerous, riders should wear helmets, pads, and gloves.

After You Read

9. Was your purpose for reading met? ____ yes ____ no

10. What new things did you learn from the passage?

_____

_____

11. How is a hoverboard different from most other kinds of transportation?

_____

_____

12. Why do you think the writer of the passage wrote it?

Ⓐ to tell how hoverboards work

Ⓑ to get readers to buy hoverboards

Ⓒ to tell people how risky hoverboards are

Ⓓ to tell people to ride hoverboards

LESSON 12   Adjusting Reading Rate

Read Fast or Read Slow?

Some kinds of writing should be read more slowly than others. You should read a passage more slowly if it:

- contains information new to you
- has a lot of unfamiliar words or long sentences
- includes technical language

To **adjust your reading rate** means to change how fast you are reading, based on what you are reading. If a passage is hard, slow down. If it's easy, speed up.

Try It Out

The passage below contains facts and technical words, like **angle, degree, and hull**. How do you think you should read this passage?

___ more quickly   ___ more slowly

Land Sailing—NONFICTION

Land yachts are vessels that sail on land. The sport of land sailing is exciting because the yachts can go at very fast speeds. Land yachts can go much faster than the wind.

A land yacht race must take place in a large open space. The land must be very flat. Land sailing can be done on beaches, in dry lake beds, or on ice or snow. Like a sailboat, a land yacht has a mast, a sail, and a hull. Unlike water boats, land yachts have only a single seat and three wheels.

In light winds, on a perfectly smooth ice surface, ice yachts can go 8 times the speed of the wind. Other land yachts can go 5 times wind speed. They go the fastest when the wind hits the sail at almost a right angle. This means the wind must hit the sail anywhere from 45 to 85 degrees off the stern, or back end, of the boat.

After You Read

1. What is a land yacht?_____

2. What can move faster, the wind or a land yacht? _____

3. What part of a land yacht is the **stern**? _____

4. Another word for **vessels** is _____.

Ⓐ masts   Ⓑ speeds   Ⓒ winds   Ⓓ boats

WORDS TO KNOW
yacht
vessels
mast
hull
angle
degrees
stern

Try It Again

The next passage is the first part of a **fiction** story about a land yacht race. This passage doesn't contain technical terms. How do you think you should read the passage? ___ more quickly ___ more slowly

Now read the passage.

Race Day—FICTION

Pat put on his helmet and stepped into the cockpit of his three-wheeled racing boat. He turned to face the gusting Nevada wind, feeling out its speed. The dry lake stretched without a tree or plant for miles around. Its only surface was flat, cracked mud. Seventeen land yachts were lined up on the surface. The yachts' colorful sails stood out against the tan background and clear blue sky.

Pat spotted Neil Bates and his red land yacht about 50 feet away. Neil was the best land yacht racer around, and he never let anyone forget it. "Maybe this time I will beat that kid," Pat said to himself. It was about time someone put "Neil the heel" in his place.

"This wind is perfect," Pat thought. "It's blowing about 25 miles per hour from the west. With luck, my boat will zoom at 60 to 70 miles per hour." He stepped into the cockpit of his three-wheeled boat.

After You Read

5. What is the story about? _____

_____

6. Whom does Pat want to beat in the race? Why?

_____

_____

7. Did you find it easier or harder to read than the passage on page 37? Why?

_____

_____

Adjusting Reading Rate While You Read

Some reading selections contain a mix of hard and easy sentences. When you come to a harder section, slow down. Then speed up again when the sentences get easier.

LESSON 13   Strategies During Reading

Keeping Track

Good readers keep track of how well they understand what they are reading. If you come to something you don't understand, take note of it instead of just reading on. Try to clear up your confusion. In this lesson you will learn three strategies for clearing up confusion while you read.

Strategy 1: Reading Ahead

Read this passage. Then answer the questions below.

It was Hasan's second week of work as a stevedore on the docks of Oakland, California. He knew that Monday would be a long day. Two hundred shipping containers were stacked on the dock. A cargo ship was waiting alongside the dock. All the containers had to be loaded onto that ship. Hasan was feeling fresh and strong. He put on his hard hat and joined the other dock workers.

STRATEGY BUILDER

Reading Ahead
If you come to something you don't understand while you're reading, try **reading ahead**. Information that comes later in the passage may clear up your confusion.

1. If you were confused by the word **stevedore** in the first sentence, how could reading ahead help you clear up your confusion?

_____

_____

2. Where did you find the information that helped you figure out the meaning of **stevedore**?

   Ⓐ in a dictionary   Ⓒ in sentences 3-5

   Ⓑ in the first sentence   Ⓓ in the last sentence

3. What is the most likely meaning of **stevedore,** based on the passage?

   Ⓐ a shipping container   Ⓒ a dock worker

   Ⓑ a cargo ship   Ⓓ a kind of hat

Now read this passage. Then answer the questions on page 40.

Hasan liked working on container ships—he liked it a lot. Loading a container ship was easy, compared to his last job. Cargo was loaded into big steel boxes called containers. All the containers were the same size, so they stacked up neatly, one on top of another. On his last job, Hasan worked for a shipping company that did not use containers. Each item had to be packed on the ship by hand, one thing at a time. Because cargo comes in all different sizes, loading and unloading this kind of ship was a big job. It took a lot of time. Hasan had made up his mind—container ships were the way to go.

4. The second sentence in the passage says "Loading a container ship was easy." If you didn't understand how loading containers onto a ship could be easy, what could you do?

Ⓐ Call up a stevedore and ask.

Ⓑ Go down to the docks and find out.

Ⓒ Read ahead to see if this is explained.

Ⓓ Look up **container** in the dictionary.

5. Underline the sentences that explain why loading a container ship is easier than loading a ship that does not use containers.

Strategy 2: Rereading

Read this passage. Then answer the questions below.

Tankers are ships made to carry one kind of cargo—oil. A tanker ship is like a big floating tank. Small tankers carry about 2,000 tons of oil. Supertankers can carry more than 450,000 tons of oil. They cannot stop or turn quickly. It costs less to ship a lot of oil in a supertanker than to send the same amount of oil in many small tankers. But supertankers pose problems, too. Their huge size puts them at greater risk for accidents. And an oil spill from a supertanker can be far more harmful than an oil spill from a smaller tanker.

6. If you didn't understand why an oil spill from a supertanker can be more harmful than an oil spill from a smaller tanker, how could rereading clear up the confusion?

_____

_____

7. Which detail below explains why an oil spill in a supertanker can be so bad?

Ⓐ A tanker is made to carry one kind of cargo.

Ⓑ Small tankers carry about 2,000 tons of oil.

Ⓒ A supertanker carries more than 450,000 tons of oil.

Ⓓ It costs less to ship a lot of oil in a supertanker.

8. Underline the sentence that gives this detail.

Strategy 3: Self-Questioning

Read this passage. Then answer the questions below.

On March 16, 1978, a supertanker named the *Amoco Cadiz* lost her steering off the coast of France. The huge ship crashed into the rocky shore. In the days that followed, almost 70 million gallons of black, sticky oil spilled into the sea. The oil spill spelled disaster for sea life.

STRATEGY BUILDER

Self-Questioning
If you come to an idea you don't understand, try asking yourself a question, and then answering it.

9. If you weren't sure what kinds of sea life were affected by the oil spill, what question might you ask yourself?

   Ⓐ Why do supertankers carry oil, if it's so risky?

   Ⓑ Which is bigger, a clam or a lobster?

   Ⓒ How big is the biggest supertanker ever made?

   Ⓓ What kinds of plants and animals live in and near the sea?

10. If you didn't understand why the oil spill spelled disaster for sea life, what question might you ask yourself?

    Ⓐ What is the biggest kind of sea life?

    Ⓑ Why might oil be bad for sea life?

    Ⓒ What does a shark look like?

    Ⓓ Who needs oil?

11. Why do you think an oil spill means disaster for sea life?

    _____

    _____

    _____

    _____

    _____

LESSON 14   Using Resources to Clarify

Going Outside the Text

As you read, you may come to something you just can't figure out. Sometimes you need to go outside the text to clear up your confusion.

Read this passage. Then answer the questions below.

The Old Days

I knew it would be my last visit to the *Atlantic Pride*. The old ship was about to be torn apart and made into scrap metal. I wanted to remember her as she used to be, decks filled with sailors and holds filled with cargo. I walked abaft the main mast, to the bridge of the old ship. There, Captain Louie had spent 22 years at the helm. As I walked the deck from stern to bow, I could not help but think of him. I'll never forget how he used to yell, "Go aft, boys!"

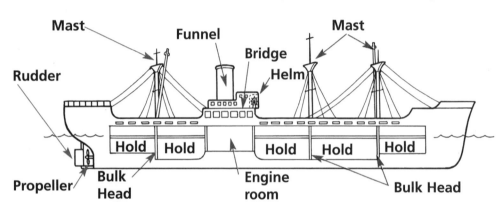

SPELLING BUILDER

You can't look up a word in the dictionary if you don't know how to spell it. Here's a tip: Write down two or three of your best guesses and look up each one until you find the word you're looking for.

Using a Dictionary

1. What does **abaft** mean? There are no context clues to help you figure it out, and the word abaft is not in the diagram. Look in a dictionary. What does **abaft** mean?

   Ⓐ in front of

   Ⓒ to the left of

   Ⓑ in the middle of

   Ⓓ to the rear of

Using Diagrams and Labels

2. Where are the **holds** of the boat? The text doesn't say where they are, but the diagram **shows it**. Look at the diagram and labels. Where are the **holds**?

   Ⓐ on top of the bridge

   Ⓒ at the bottom of the ship

   Ⓑ on the main mast

   Ⓓ inside the funnel

Using Human Resources

Say you don't know what **bow to stern** means. One of your teachers or a friend who knows boats can help you. Try asking the people around you to clarify what **bow to stern** means. (If you can't find the answer, look in the dictionary.)

3. What part of a ship is the **bow**? _____

4. What part of a ship is the **stern**? _____

LESSON 15   Remembering What You Read

Making Facts Stick

It's easy to forget what you read. In this lesson you'll learn three strategies for making facts stick in your head.

Read this passage about pythons.

A Giant Among Snakes Pythons are among the world's biggest snakes. Some pythons grow to a length of 30 feet. That's as long as five six-foot-tall people, lying end to end.

First Squeeze, Then Eat Pythons kill their prey by squeezing the life out of it. For this reason they are called constrictors. To constrict means "to stop the flow." First the python wraps itself around a victim. Then it squeezes until the victim stops breathing. Once the victim is dead, the python eats it.

Eating Habits Most pythons eat small animals, such as rabbits and cats. Bigger pythons sometimes eat wild pigs, which can weigh up to 100 pounds. A python eats the whole animal without chewing it. It can take many days for a python to digest a meal. As its food is digesting, a python looks odd. You can see the shape of the animal as it moves through the snake's long body.

Pythons Everywhere? You may be unhappy to know that pythons live in many places. They thrive in warm, tropical climates. Pythons can be found in parts of Asia, India, Africa, and Australia.

WORDS TO KNOW

python

prey

constrictor

digest

tropical

TEST TIP

Taking notes is a great way to prepare for a test. Reviewing your notes before a test is a good way to remember important points.

Taking Notes

One good strategy for remembering what you read is to take notes while you are reading. When you take notes, you jot down the most important ideas in a passage. Card #1 shows the notes you might take for the first two paragraphs of the passage.

On card #2, write five notes for the third and fourth paragraphs.

```
                    Pythons              1
size
  • one of the biggest snakes
  • can grow to 30 feet
how they eat
  • kill prey by wrapping around it and squeezing
  • called constrictors
  • constrict = "to stop the flow"
```

```
                                         2
1. _____
2. _____
3. _____
4. _____
5. _____
```

Talking About What You Read

One thing you can do to help yourself remember facts is to talk about what you read with a friend.

Read the conversation below. Fill in the answers that are missing.

You: I read this creepy passage about pythons.

Your Friend: What's a python?

6. You: _____
           (what)   (how big)

Your Friend: What does it eat?

7. You: _____
          (most pythons)   (bigger pythons)

Your Friend: Does it have huge fangs it can sink into you?

8. You: _____
          (how it kills)

Your Friend: That's disgusting. I'm never going on a hike again.

9. You: _____
          (where pythons do and do not live)

Rereading

A simple trick for remembering what you read is to reread a passage. (Also, rereading sometimes lets you discover a fact you missed the first time.) You can reread a passage as many times as you need to, until you are confident that you know the facts in it.

Reread the passage about pythons.

10. Did you discover any facts you missed the first time? If so, what?

_____

_____

11. Is there anything in the passage you did not understand?
____ yes   ____ no

12. If your answer is yes, tell what you could do to clear up your confusion.

_____

_____

LESSON 16   Choosing the Right Strategy

The Right Strategy for the Job

Now you know all about reading strategies. But how do you know which strategy to use, and when? This lesson will give you practice with choosing the right strategy.

Read the next passage carefully. You will use it to answer all the questions in this lesson.

Long and Lean: A Mean Machine

Different Ways of Getting Prey Constrictors kill their prey by squeezing them. Vipers and elapids kill their victims in another way. Vipers and elapids are both poisonous snakes. Vipers can fold their long fangs back when the fangs are not in use. Elapids have shorter fangs, and the fangs don't move. Poisonous snakes inject a poison called venom into their victims. The venom shoots out through a hole in the fangs called the venom duct.

How Snakes Digest Food Most snakes eat their victims alive. But how does a snake get its mouth around a victim that is bigger than it is? Snakes can unhinge their jaws and open their mouths very, very wide. As an animal is digested, a snake's ribs expand. Its scales stretch apart, too. This allows the victim to pass through the snake's body.

Snakes as Helpers Snakes may seem creepy, but they are useful to people in many ways. Certain painkilling drugs are made from snake venom. Venom is also used to treat people who have been bitten by snakes. The venom is mixed with horse blood to make a mix called antivenin. Most people try to stay away from snakes. If you were a maker of antivenin, though, you'd probably be happy to see a poisonous snake in your path—if you were ready for it.

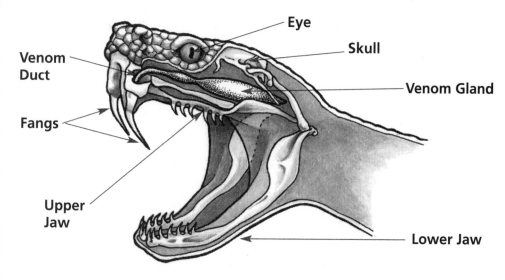

Ask Reed

Imagine that you write an advice column for a school paper. Confused readers send you questions, and you answer them. Your column is called **Ask Reed**.

Read these letters. Answer each one by suggesting a reading strategy that can clear up the writer's confusion. One has been done for you.

Strategy Menu	
• Preview and Predict	• Set a Purpose
• Adjust Reading Rate	• Reread to Clarify
• Read Ahead	• Use a Dictionary
• Use a Diagram	• Take Notes/Reread

Dear Reed,

I read that thing about snakes. Yuck! But I'm confused about one thing. How does venom get inside a snake's fang? The text didn't explain it. Can you?

Wants to Know

Dear Wants to Know,   1

No, the text did not explain how venom gets in a snake's fang. But the diagram shows how this happens. Look at the diagram. Find the venom duct and the venom gland. The picture shows how venom goes from the venom gland, through the head, and into the fangs.

Sincerely,

Reed

Dear Reed,

You know that passage about snakes? I got to the end of it and I was so mixed up. How in the world could anyone be happy to find a poisonous snake? I don't get it.

Clueless

Dear Clueless,   2

_____

_____

_____

_____

_____

Sincerely,

Reed

Dear Reed,

I came to the word **elapid** in the second sentence and it stopped me cold! I don't know that word! I put the book down, and I'm not sure I want to pick it up again.

Stumped

Dear Stumped,   **3**

_____

_____

_____

_____

Sincerely,

Reed

Dear Reed,

I got to the end of that passage about snakes and it was like I went blank. I couldn't remember a thing I'd read! Got any tips?

Forgetful

Dear Forgetful,   **4**

_____

_____

_____

_____

_____

Sincerely,

Reed

Dear Reed,

You can't believe how disgusted I am! I read that passage titled **Long and Lean: A Mean Machine**. Based on the title, I thought I was going to read about race cars, but it was all about snakes! Snakes give me the creeps! I'm sure I won't sleep for a week. How can I avoid this in the future?

Ophidiophobe

(scared of snakes)

Dear Ophi,   **5**

_____

_____

_____

_____

_____

Sincerely,

Reed

Part A

Vocabulary for Reading Strategies

VOCABULARY BUILDER

Prefixes can help you figure out word meanings. **Non-** means "not," so **nonfiction** means "not fiction." **Pre-** means "before," so **preview** means "look before."

Write each word in the box next to the word or phrase that has almost the same meaning.

nonfiction	clarify	fiction
adjust	rate	caption

1. to make clear _____

2. a made-up story _____

3. how fast _____

4. writing made up mostly of facts _____

5. make a change _____

6. words under a picture _____

TEST TIP

On most tests, every question is worth the same amount. When this is the case, you should always do the easiest questions first.

Draw a line from each word on the left to its meaning on the right.

7. prediction   • a short piece of writing

8. purpose   • a plan of attack

9. passage   • to look ahead

10. resources   • a guess about what might happen

11. strategy   • a dictionary or encyclopedia

12. preview   • your reason for reading

Part B

Strategies Before Reading

Preview the passage on page 49. Then answer questions 1–5.

1. What is the title of the passage? _____

2. What does the picture show? _____

3. Is the passage fiction or nonfiction? _____

4. What do you think the passage will be about, based on your preview?

   (A) Greek words   (C) pictures made on rocks

   (B) the American Southwest   (D) making a profit on rocks

5. What will be your purpose for reading the passage?

_____

_____

Rock Art

Pictures with Meaning For thousands of years, Native Americans have carved pictures into rocks. Rock art is found in many places throughout the American Southwest. The carvings were made for different reasons. Some carvings show where something important, such as water, can be found. Others tell the story of important events. Still others show animals the Native Americans hunted.

Two Kinds of Rock Art One kind of rock art is made by scraping or carving pictures into the rock using sharp tools. Such images are called **petroglyphs**. **Petroglyph** comes from two Greek words. **Petro** means "rock," and **glyph** means "carving." Another kind of rock art is made by coloring the rock face with paints made of things like coal, plant extracts, and blood. These images are called **pictographs**. **Picto** means "picture," and **graph** means "write."

Reading Rock Art Some images on rock are easy to see. These include images of lizards, snakes, birds, and other animals everyone knows. Understanding what these images mean often takes special knowledge, however. The snake was often associated with water. Certain birds were associated with ceremonies. It's one thing to know what a picture shows. It's another thing to understand what the picture means.

These pictures show animals, images found in the night sky, and people taking part in ceremonies.

- To **preview** is to look at a piece of writing to see what it's about.

- To **predict** is to make a guess about what might happen in a passage, based on your preview.

- To **set a purpose** is to decide why you are reading. You might read to learn facts, to find information, or just to have fun.

KEY WORDS

Native American

Southwest

petroglyph

pictograph

carvings

images

ceremonies

Part C

Strategies During Reading

If you get confused while reading, try these strategies:

- **Reread** to find a fact or detail you may have missed, or to clarify a word that was defined earlier.

- **Read ahead** to see if the next part of the passage clears up your confusion by giving an explanation or word meaning.

- **Use a resource** such as a dictionary to look up a word.

- **Ask yourself questions.**

Read the following passage. Then answer the questions.

No one knows for sure what the images in petroglyphs and pictographs mean. The people who study rock art have come up with many different ideas about what rock artists were trying to say.

a

Animals
Pictures like these may have been made to draw animals out of their hiding places, making it easier to hunt them.

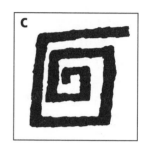
c

A New Home
This image may have told viewers that the clan or tribe had found a new home.

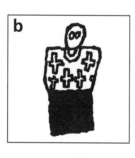
b

Life-Size Images of People
Pictures like this one may show a leader who died. Perhaps the image was supposed to let the leader's spirit pass in and out of the rock whenever it wanted to.

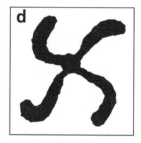
d

Migration
Many Southwest tribes believed that their people came up out of a hole in the earth. From there, they moved north, south, east, and west. This image may have been created to show the first migration.

1. If you were stumped by the words **petroglyph** and **pictograph** in the first sentence, what could you do?

   _____

   _____

2. About how tall were the pictures of leaders who had died?

   Ⓐ 2 feet tall   Ⓒ 10 feet tall

   Ⓑ 5 feet tall   Ⓓ 20 feet tall

3. Where did you find that information?

   _____

4. Find the word **Migration** next to the fourth picture. If you were confused by this word's meaning, what could you do? Check one box and explain why you would use that strategy.

☐ Reread, because _____

_____

☐ Read ahead, because _____

_____

5. The word **spirit** is not explained in the text. What could you do to find the meaning of this word?

_____

_____

Remembering What You Read

Part D

In the space below, write the notes you would take for the passage on page 50.

first paragraph: _____

_____

_____

picture a: _____

_____

picture b: _____

_____

picture c: _____

_____

picture d: _____

_____

- **Rereading** can help you remember what you read.

- **Taking notes** can help you understand and remember main ideas.

- **Talking about what you read** is a good way of making facts stick in your mind.

Introduction

In school, your purpose for reading is often to learn new facts and practice skills. There are many reasons to read outside of school, too. Read the list below. Write **S** next to the tasks that have to do with school. Write **O** next to the things that have to do with other parts of life.

_____ Study for a test about Egypt.

_____ Find out where the movie *Mummy Curse* is playing.

_____ Look for a part-time job.

_____ Find the phone number of the Mummy Museum.

_____ Book an airplane ticket to Cairo, Egypt.

_____ Get facts for your report about King Tut.

_____ Compare prices of athletic shoes.

_____ Find a recipe for fudge.

Print Is Everywhere!

Print is all around us, all the time. Every kind of printed matter has a purpose. Thinking about the purpose of a piece of writing can help you understand what you read. Read the list on the left. Then draw a line from each kind of printed material to its purpose.

Print	Purpose
newspaper	keep us safe
ad	get us to buy something
schedule	explain what we're eating
food product label	tell us how to cook something
recipe	tell us when events will happen
warning label	report what's going on in the world

In real life, reading can help you get the best deal, stay informed, and get you where you are going. Chapter 3 will help you understand and use the print you find in everyday life.

LESSON 17   Staying Informed

Newspapers

Newspapers give up-to-date news about what's going on in the world. **Local newspapers** give information about the city where they are published. **National newspapers** are read all over the country. Newspapers are usually published every day or every week. Newspapers are organized into sections by topic. All the main topics covered in a newspaper are listed in the **index**. The index tells you what part of the paper each topic is covered in.

WORDS TO KNOW

newspapers

section

index

alphabetical

headlines

Look at the following newspaper index. Then answer the questions.

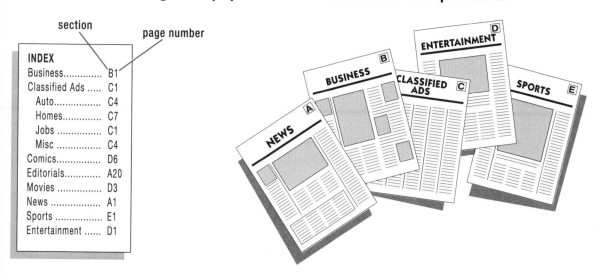

section   page number

INDEX
Business.............. B1
Classified Ads C1
  Auto................ C4
  Homes............. C7
  Jobs C1
  Misc C4
Comics................ D6
Editorials............. A20
Movies D3
News A1
Sports E1
Entertainment D1

1. How is this index set up? Fill in the correct circle.

   Ⓐ from most important topic to least important topic

   Ⓑ section A comes first, followed by B, C, D, and E

   Ⓒ in alphabetical order by topic

   Ⓓ in no order at all

2. On which section and page would you find football scores?
   section _____, page _____

3. Where would you look for a car? section _____, page _____

4. What does the word **Misc.** under Classified Ads mean?

   Ⓐ mister   Ⓒ muscle

   Ⓑ miscellaneous   Ⓓ music

Reading the Paper

People usually don't read the newspaper from beginning to end. Instead, they look at **headlines** and read the articles that interest them.

Read each headline below. Then draw a line to match the headline with the section where you'd find it.

5. President Visits Mexico   Business B1

6. FOR SALE: Pizza Oven   Entertainment D1

7. Bisons Beat Bats; Fans Go Rabid   News A1

8. *Mad Mummy* Beats Box Office Record   Sports E1

9. Small Company Makes Big Bucks   Classified Ads C1

Missing Snake Makes Town Nervous

Residents in Oaktown may not sleep very well tonight. An 8-foot-long snake is on the loose. The runaway is a bull snake named Rocky. He escaped yesterday from the Oaktown Zoo.

"There is really nothing to be afraid of," said zoo warden Mike Fierro. "Rocky is not dangerous. He is just very big."

The snake slipped out of its cage during feeding time on Friday morning.

The feeder, Dawn Rhodes, was bringing Rocky his morning meal of mice, so the cage door was open.

Then a fight broke out between two iguanas. The feeder turned around and yelled at the iguanas. "I only turned my back for a minute," she said. "When I looked back at the cage, Rocky was gone!"

Zoo workers and local police have been looking for Rocky in the park. They think he may be hiding in a hole. If you see Rocky or know where he might be, please call the police at 555-3456.

How to Read a News Story

Most newspaper articles answer these six questions: Who? What? When? Where? Why? and How?

Read the news article about the missing snake. Then follow the directions below.

10. Circle **who** the story is about.

11. Underline **what** happened.

12. Draw two lines under **when** it happened.

13. Draw a dotted line under **where** it happened.

14. Draw a box around **why** it happened.

15. Then put a star by **how** it happened.

News on the Internet

Many newspapers are published on the Internet. The top stories of the day are listed on the first screen you come to. Click on a story to read it. An online newspaper lets you do one important thing that regular newspapers do not—search for news articles from the past. If you want to find every article a newspaper printed about bull snakes, you can type **bull snakes** into a box and click on the **Search** button. The titles of the articles will appear on the screen.

LESSON 18   Finding Facts

Looking for Information

Being able to find information is a powerful skill. Here are two things that will help you find information fast: 1) Know where to look. 2) Know what to look for.

Where to Look

Knowing where to look for information is the first step. Here are some reference sources that people use every day:

Reference Source	What You Find There
encyclopedia	general information on topics from **A** to **Z**
almanac	up-to-date facts and data
atlas	maps of different parts of the world
phone book	local phone numbers and addresses
Internet	news, facts, and opinions

What to Look For

When you want to find information, think about the **key words** that might lead you to that information. For example, if you are looking for information on fashion styles of the 1970s, you could try the key words **fashion, clothing,** or **designers**. Then use alphabetical order to look up the words in the reference source you chose.

Read the questions below. Then read the possible key words. Fill in the circle for the key word that would probably lead you to each answer.

1. How many Godzilla movies were made?

Ⓐ movies   Ⓒ tickets

Ⓑ scary   Ⓓ Godzilla

2. Who hit the most home runs in a single season?

Ⓐ baseball   Ⓒ season

Ⓑ sports   Ⓓ bats

3. How does a TV work?

Ⓐ entertainment Ⓒ electricity

Ⓑ television   Ⓓ work

WORDS TO KNOW

reference

encyclopedia

almanac

atlas

Internet

key word

READING TIP

Alphabetical Order
In most reference sources, subjects appear in alphabetical order. To find **Godzilla**, go past the pages that list topics beginning with **a, b, c, d, e,** and **f**. If there is an entry for **Godzilla**, it will appear after **f** and before **h**. Many reference sources have a **guide word** at the top of each page. It tells you what letter the entries on that page start with.

Searching on the Internet

People use **search engines** to look for information on the Internet. You type a key word, and the computer searches for information. Sometimes it finds articles with information, and sometimes it finds Web sites where you can look for more information. Here are the basics of searching for information on the Internet:

- Type a key word in the search box. (Hint: A search engine often finds thousands of sources of information! Make your search more specific by typing more than one key word.)
- Click on the search button.
- Look at the **search results,** and read the underlined links.
- Click on a link that looks useful.

Let's say you want to learn some new hip-hop dance moves. You type the key words **dance videos** and click on the **Search** button. Here's what you get.

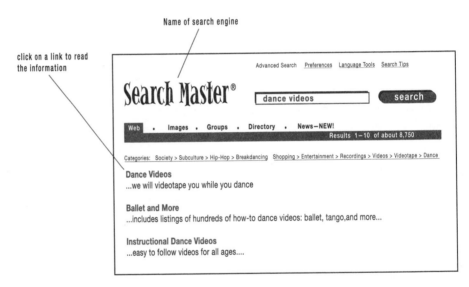

STRATEGY BUILDER

There are two ways to get information on the Internet:

- Do a key word search.
- Type the name of a Web site.

4. You don't have time to read 8,750 bits of information! You need to use more specific key words. Mark the key word or phrase that could help narrow your search.

   Ⓐ hip-hop music   Ⓒ weekend

   Ⓑ hip-hop videos   Ⓓ lessons

5. Say you want information about keeping a bull snake as a pet. Which key words would you use?

   Ⓐ **snakes** and **animals**   Ⓒ **crazy** and **reptile**

   Ⓑ **pets** and **animals**   Ⓓ **bull snakes** and **pets**

6. What key words would you use if you wanted information about sports camps? _____ and _____

Using a Telephone Book

The telephone book lists local telephone numbers in two ways.

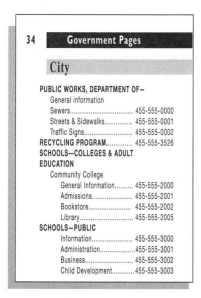

White Pages list people and companies by name in alphabetical order. In many phone books there are three sections in the White Pages: government listings, business listings, and residence (home) listings.

Yellow Pages group businesses, organizations, and services by type. Then they list them by name in alphabetical order. Yellow pages also contain ads.

Yellow Pages or White Pages?

Let's say you want to find the phone number of a restaurant that delivers pizza. Should you use the yellow pages or the white pages? It depends.

- If you know the name of the restaurant, you can look it up in the business section of the white pages using alphabetical order. For example, Fire Chief Pizza would be listed with other words starting with **f**.
- If you don't know the name of the restaurant, use the yellow pages. Look up **restaurants** under **r**. Then scan through the listings and the ads. Look for a pizza restaurant that delivers.

7. You want to find the phone number of a store that sells baseball cleats and basketballs. You don't know the name of the store. Where should you look? Why? ___ yellow pages ___ white pages

because: _____

8. What key word would you look up to find the listings for stores that might sell baseball cleats and basketballs?

Ⓐ **sports,** under **s**

Ⓒ **baseball,** under **b**

Ⓑ **fashion,** under **f**

Ⓓ **business,** under **b**

LESSON 19   Giving Information About Yourself

WORDS TO KNOW

application

employment

position

experience

Completing an Application

When applying for a job, a credit card, or membership in a club, you usually need to give facts about yourself. You might be given an **application form** to fill out.

Read this form. Did the person who filled it out make any mistakes? Circle each mistake you find.

APPLICATION FOR EMPLOYMENT
BART'S BURGER BARN

Date _Next Monday_

Name: _Lance   Evan   Green_   Telephone _$8 an hour, if I can get it_
         (LAST)   (FIRST)   (M.I.)

Address: _2022 Berringer St._
         (#)   (STREET)   (CITY)   (STATE)   (ZIP CODE)

EMPLOYMENT DESIRED   Date you   Salary
                                            can start _8 A.M._   Desired _____
Position _I don't like to stand up all day long._

EDUCATION	Years Attended	Degree	Best Subjects
High School _Beaumont High_	From _____ To _____	☐ yes ☐ no	all
College _not yet_			
WORK EXPERIENCE Name and location of firm	Date Started	Date Left	Position
Walt's Weenie World			

Why would you make a good employee at Bart's Burger Barn? List two reasons.
1. _I'm broke_
2. _I like burgers._

Special skills or abilities you possess:
  I am five foot ten. I have brown eyes and red hair.

Your Signature _____

SPELLING BUILDER

Double check the spelling of names when you write. Names are easy to misspell.

1. What probably belongs next to the word **Date**?_____

2. Read the words in small type under the line where the name belongs. Lance made two mistakes when he wrote his name. Write his name the way it should have been written.

_____

3. In a job application, the word **Position** means "job." What did Lance write next to **Position**?

_____

4. What should he have written there?

Ⓐ the name of the job he wants

Ⓑ what position he is in as he fills out the application

Ⓒ where he plans to be tomorrow

Ⓓ his name and address

5. By asking what subjects people were best at in school, bosses are trying to find out what interests job applicants and what they might be good at. Under **Best Subjects,** Lance wrote **all**. What would have been a better answer?

Ⓐ none

Ⓒ the two classes he liked best

Ⓑ rocket science

Ⓓ lunch

6. The application asks people to list reasons why they would be good workers at Bart's Burgers. What did Lance do wrong here?

_____

_____

7. Fill in the circles for two reasons that would be good answers to this question.

Ⓐ I am a hard worker and I like people.

Ⓑ I love the idea of getting free burgers.

Ⓒ I have worked at a restaurant before.

Ⓓ Bart's Burgers needs somebody who actually knows how to cook a burger.

8. Did Lance fill in the last item, "Special skills or abilities you possess," correctly? Why or why not?

___ yes ___ no

because _____

Try Your Hand

Fill out the application below. Try not to make the same mistakes Lance did.

APPLICATION FOR EMPLOYMENT
BART'S BURGER BARN

Date _____

Name: _____ Telephone _____
      (LAST)   (FIRST)   (M.I.)

Address: _____
    (#)   (STREET)   (CITY)   (STATE)   (ZIP CODE)

EMPLOYMENT DESIRED   Date you   Salary

                         can start _____ Desired _____

Position _____

EDUCATION	Years Attended	Degree	Best Subjects
High School	From _____ To _____	☐ yes ☐ no	
College	From _____ To _____	☐ yes ☐ no	

WORK EXPERIENCE Name and location of firm	Date Started_____	Date Left_____	Position

Why would you make a good employee at Bart's Burger Barn? List two reasons.

1. _____

2. _____

Special skills or abilities you possess:

                Your Signature_____

WRITING TIP

Before turning in an application, read it again carefully. Look for mistakes in spelling or capitalization. Fix any mistakes you find. Also make sure your writing is easy to read.

LESSON 20   Following Directions

Step–by–Step

Directions tell you how to do something. The steps to follow are usually given in the order they should be done. **Sequence words** such as **first, next,** and **last** can help you understand the order of the steps.

WORDS TO KNOW

directions

sequence

recipe

ingredients

visual

Read a Recipe

Read this recipe. Pay attention to the sequence of steps.

Chocolate Chip Cookies

To bake chocolate chip cookies, you will need the following ingredients:

1 stick unsalted butter	1 egg
6 tablespoons sugar	1 cup flour
6 tablespoons light brown sugar	$\frac{1}{2}$ teaspoon baking soda
$\frac{1}{4}$ teaspoon salt	1 cup chocolate chips
$1\frac{1}{2}$ teaspoons vanilla extract	1 cup pecans or walnuts (optional)

First preheat the oven to 375 degrees F. Then mix the butter, sugars, salt, and vanilla until blended well. Beat in the egg to this mixture. In a different bowl, mix together the flour and baking soda. Next, add the dry ingredients to the wet ingredients and mix. Stir in the chocolate chips and nuts. Then shape the batter into small balls and place them on an ungreased baking sheet. Bake for 9-12 minutes, or until cookies are golden brown. Let the cookies cool before eating them. (This recipe makes about $2\frac{1}{2}$ dozen cookies.)

Think About Sequence

These steps below for making cookies are in the wrong order!

1–5. Write 1–5 on the lines to show when each step should be done.

_____ Add the egg to the wet ingredients.

_____ Mix the wet and dry ingredients together.

_____ Place cookies in the oven.

_____ Add chocolate chips.

_____ Preheat the oven.

Underline three sequence words in the recipe. Then write the words on the lines below.

6. _____

7. _____

8. _____

9. The directions say, "Bake for 9-12 minutes, or until the cookies are golden brown." What does this sentence tell you?

Ⓐ All ovens are exactly the same.

Ⓑ It is wrong to bake cookies that are golden brown.

Ⓒ 9-12 minutes is too long to wait for cookies.

Ⓓ Some ovens cook things faster than others.

Visual Directions

Some directions come with pictures. These directions show and tell how to insert a battery and a memory card into a digital camera.

Read the directions and look at the pictures.

Inserting the Battery

Your digital camera comes with a battery that can be recharged. You must charge the battery before you put it in the camera. Use the battery charger that came with your camera.

1. Turn the camera off.

2. Slide the battery-chamber latch to the open position and flip the cover open.

3. Insert the battery.

4. Close the battery chamber cover and close the latch.

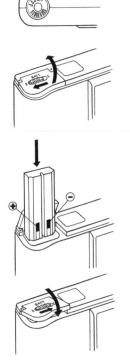

Insert the Memory Card

1. Before you insert the memory card, make sure the camera is off.

2. Slide the card-slot cover out (a) and flip it open (b). Make sure the arrow on the card faces towards you. Insert the card in the direction of the arrow (c). Slide the card until it is in place and the eject button pops up. Close the slot card cover (d).

(a,b)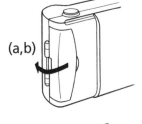

(c)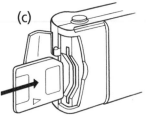

(d)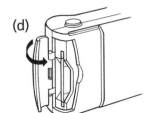

Think About Sequence

10. What is the FIRST thing you should do before inserting the battery?

    ___ Turn off the camera.

    ___ Open the battery chamber.

    ___ Charge the battery.

11. What should you do AFTER inserting the memory card?

    ___ Insert the battery.

    ___ Close the slot cover.

    ___ Turn the camera off.

12. What do the second set of pictures help you understand?

    Ⓐ how to put in a memory card

    Ⓑ which direction to put the battery in

    Ⓒ which is the OFF position

    Ⓓ how a memory card is made

13. Circle the picture that shows what you do after you've inserted the memory card.

VOCABULARY BUILDER

Along with new technology comes new words for talking about these products. You can look up unfamiliar words in the glossary or index of an instruction manual, or in a dictionary.

LESSON 21   Reading Schedules

WORDS TO KNOW

schedule

column

headings

Keeping Track of Time

When does the train to Cleveland leave? What time does the play start? How long will this class last? Schedules answer all these questions. Schedules tell when events happen.

Read a Schedule

Cora has a new job after school. She made this schedule to keep track of her time.

Look at Cora's schedule. Then answer the questions.

	Monday	Tuesday	Wednesday	Thursday	Friday
8:00–9:00		swimming		swimming	
9:00–10:00	school	school	school	school	school
10:00–11:00					
11:00–12:00					
12:00–1:00					
1:00–2:00					
2:00–3:00		homework		homework	
3:00–4:00					
4:00–5:00	pick up sister	take sister to babysitter	pick up sister	take sister to babysitter	pick up sister
5:00–6:00	cook dinner		cook dinner		cook dinner
6:00–7:00					
7:00–8:00	homework	work	homework	work	see movie!
8:00–9:00					

STRATEGY BUILDER

Look for the word **work** in the schedule. Then look up at the column headings to find the days of the week.

1. On which days does Cora work after school? Fill in the corrrect circle.

Ⓐ Monday, Wednesday, and Friday

Ⓑ Tuesday and Thursday

Ⓒ every day

Ⓓ Tuesday and Wednesday

2. What task must Cora do every day after school?

_____

3. How many hours does Cora spend at school on Wednesday?

   Ⓐ four   Ⓒ six

   Ⓑ five   Ⓓ eight

4–7. When does Cora make time for fun in her busy week?

              Swimming   **Movie**

Time: _____   Time: _____

Days:_____   Day: _____

THINK ABOUT IT

Think about why people use schedules. When are schedules the most helpful? When are they least helpful? Is keeping a schedule worth the time it takes to make and update it? Why or why not?

Now look at Cora's weekend schedule. Then answer the questions.

	Saturday	Sunday
10:00-11:00	school car wash	work
11:00-12:00	school car wash	work
12:00-1:00	school car wash	work
1:00-2:00		work
2:00-3:00	work	work
3:00-4:00	work	work
4:00-5:00	work	work
5:00-6:00	work	
6:00-7:00	Grandmother's birthday party	B
7:00-8:00	Grandmother's birthday party	B
8:00-9:00		B
9:00-10:00	A	B
10:00-11:00	A	

8. Cora needs four hours on either Saturday or Sunday to do homework. Which time slot would be better? Circle one.

   Time slot A   **Time slot B**

9. Cora wants to work one more hour on either Saturday or Sunday. Which of these times is she free to work?

   Ⓐ 6:00-7:00 on Saturday   Ⓒ anytime on Saturday

   Ⓑ 4:00-5:00 on Sunday   Ⓓ 10:00-11:00 on Saturday

Catching the Bus

Cora needs to take the bus to her new job. Cora's school is at Mission and 16th Street. Her job is at Mission and Elm.

Look at the bus schedule below. Then answer the questions.

Bus 38
Afternoon Schedule: Monday–Friday

Mission & 24th	Mission & 16th	Mission & 8th	Mission & 1st	Mission & Davis	Mission & Elm	Mission & Main
2:00	2:05	2:10	2:15	2:20	2:25	2:30
2:20	2:25	2:30	2:35	2:40	2:45	2:50
2:40	2:45	2:50	2:55	3:00	3:05	3:10
3:00	3:05	3:10	3:15	3:20	3:25	3:30
3:20	3:25	3:30	3:35	3:40	3:45	3:50
3:40	3:45	3:50	3:55	4:00	4:05	4:10
4:00	4:05	4:10	4:15	4:20	4:25	4:30
4:20	4:25	4:30	4:35	4:40	4:45	4:50
4:40	4:45	4:50	4:55	5:00	5:05	5:10
5:00	5:05	5:10	5:15	5:20	5:25	5:30
5:20	5:25	5:30	5:35	5:40	5:45	5:50
6:00	6:05	6:10	6:15	6:20	6:25	6:30
6:20	6:25	6:30	6:35	6:40	6:45	6:50

10. If Cora catches the 5:05 bus from Mission and 16th, what time will she arrive at Mission and Elm? _____

11. Cora starts work at 6 p.m. Which is the last bus she can catch at Mission and 16th in order to make it to work on time? _____

12. Figure out how long it takes Cora to get to work by bus.

Time she arrives at work: _____

Time she catches the bus: −   _____

             =   _____ Time on the bus

13. If you wanted to get to Mission and Main at 4:30, which bus could you take from Mission and 24th?

Ⓐ ___ 3:30   Ⓒ ___ 4:00

Ⓑ ___ 3:50   Ⓓ ___ 4:25

LESSON 22   Thinking Critically: Being a Smart Consumer

Think Before You Buy

We are all consumers. We buy and use things on a daily basis. We make decisions about what to buy. These decisions can affect our health and well-being. That's why it is important to be a smart consumer.

Smart Consumer Checklist
____ Think critically about what you read, see, and hear.
____ Gather all the facts you can. Read product labels.
____ Ask whether you can trust the source of information.
____ Be aware of what is fact and what is not.
____ Take time to consider the facts and make your decision.

WORDS TO KNOW

consumer

advertising

appeal

message

government

Think Critically About Ads

Every day you see dozens of ads—on billboards, on buses, on TV, and in the news. Do you stop to think about the ads you see? Advertising companies know a lot about the way people think. They write ads that appeal to human needs and desires. Ads often contain "hidden messages" you don't even know you are getting. Here are some things that ads often appeal to:

☐ **hunger or thirst**—A soft drink ad shows a close-up of a fit-looking runner drinking a cold drink on a hot day.

☐ **desire for wealth**—A car ad shows people driving an expensive car, wearing expensive clothes, and smiling.

☐ **desire for good health**—An ad for running shoes shows lean, fit, attractive people. They are running up a hill.

☐ **desire for love**—A jewelry ad shows a woman wearing a diamond ring and smiling up at her husband.

Write the number of each hidden message in the box above, next to the ad it fits best.

1. If you buy that for your wife, she'll love you even more!

2. If you get one of these, you'll be rich and happy, too.

3. Drinking one of these will cool you off and make you fit.

4. Buy a pair of these and you will look slim and fit in no time!

How can we avoid spending money on things that don't help us much? First, we can think about how ads appeal to our desires.

Try out your critical thinking skills on this ad. Read the ad to the left. Look for facts. Then answer the questions.

5. What is the purpose of this ad?

   Ⓐ to get you to buy the soda

   Ⓑ to give facts about a soda

   Ⓒ to tell what's in the soda

   Ⓓ to make you feel rich

6. Fill in the circle for the statements that are facts:

   Ⓐ Drinking Fresh Mist is a thrilling experience.

   Ⓑ Fresh Mist is soda.

   Ⓒ Fresh Mist tastes like a mountain stream.

   Ⓓ The bottle holds 20 ounces of soda.

7. What is the ad probably appealing to? (Check two.)

   Ⓐ desire for wealth

   Ⓑ a basic need—quenching thirst

   Ⓒ desire for excitement

   Ⓓ a basic need—satisfying hunger

Reading Product Labels

Government rules say that certain information must appear on the labels of food, medicines, and other products. A good way of getting facts about the products you buy is to read the labels.

Look at the food label. Then answer the questions on page 69.

Product Name

Health Information

Weight of the Food in the Box

Last Date the Store Should Sell the Food

8. Circle how much the food in the box weighs.

9. What health information do you see on the label? _____

10. What is the latest date you should buy this product? _____

Important information appears on the sides and back of food packages. It tells what the food is made of and what vitamins, minerals, and other nutrients it contains. The package should also tell consumers how to contact the company that makes the food, in case they have questions or problems.

Look at the nutrition facts from the side of the macaroni and cheese box. Then answer the questions.

11. Underline the number of servings that the box contains.

12. How many fat calories are in each serving? _____

13. How many fat calories would you eat if you ate the whole box? _____

The chart at the bottom of the label tells how much fat, salt, cholesterol, and fiber you should eat in a day. The chart assumes that most people eat 2,000-2,500 calories in a day.

14. What is the largest amount of fat a person should eat in a day?

• Based on 2,000 calories: _____

• Based on 2,500 calories: _____

15. Sodium is salt. What is the largest amount of salt a person should have in a day?

• Based on 2,000 calories: _____

• Based on 2,500 calories: _____

16. A serving of macaroni and cheese has 18% of the fat and 20% of the sodium a person should eat in a day, based on a 2,000-calorie diet. Circle the two places on the label that give this information.

Don't worry if you don't understand every word on a nutrition label. If you take time to read labels, little by little you will become familiar with what things different foods contain. This will make you a smarter consumer. For more information on good nutrition, talk to a doctor or a nutrition expert.

Nutrition Facts		
Serving Size 1 cup (70g)		
Servings Per Container 3		
Amount Per Serving		
Calories 250	Calories from Fat 110	
		% Daily Value*
Total Fat 12g		18%
Saturated Fat 3g		15%
Cholesterol 30mg		10%
Sodium 470mg		20%
Total Carbohydrate 31g		10%
Dietary Fiber 0g		0%
Sugars 5g		
Protein 5g		
Vitamin A 4%	•	Vitamin C 2%
Calcium 20%	•	Iron 4%

*Percent Daily Values are based on a 2,000 calorie diet. Your daily values may be higher or lower depending on your calorie needs.

	Calories:	2,000	2,500
Total Fat	Less than	65 g	80g
Sat Fat	Less than	20g	25g
Cholesterol	Less than	300mg	300mg
Sodium	Less than	2,400mg	2,400mg
Total Carbohydrate		300 g	375g
Dietary Fiber		25 g	30g

Calories per gram:
Fat 9 • Carbohydrate 4 • Protein 4

Part A   Finding and Thinking About Information

Draw a line to match each source of information with one reason people use it. One is done for you.

1. search engine	find out what you need to cook something
2. classified ads	list the jobs you have had before
3. telephone directory	find the phone number of a person
4. job application	find out how much fat is in a serving of food
5. bus schedule	find information on the Internet by typing a key word
6. list of ingredients	find a used car for sale
7. food label	find out how often a bus runs

Look at the newspaper index. Then answer the questions.

Index	
Business	B1
Classifieds	C1
Comics	D6
Editorials	A20
Food	F1
Movies	D3
Sports	E1
Travel	D8
TV	D1

8. In which section might you find a cookie recipe?

    Ⓐ   Ⓑ   Ⓒ   Ⓓ   Ⓔ   Ⓕ

9. In which section could you find job listings?

    Ⓐ   Ⓑ   Ⓒ   Ⓓ   Ⓔ   Ⓕ

10. Where could you find information about train or airplane tickets?

    Section _____, page _____

Are YOU planning a vacation getaway with that special person?

HOP ON BOARD the Dream Boat. You'll have the vacation of your dreams — one you'll remember for a lifetime.

We sail every week to Mexico • Alaska • Europe • Bermuda

Call 888-555-4HUG for more details.

Read this travel ad. Then answer the questions.

11. Circle each fact you see in the ad.

12. Underline the sentence that makes a promise the company may not be able to keep.

13. What human need does this ad appeal to?

    Ⓐ our need for money

    Ⓑ our need for good health

    Ⓒ our need for love

    Ⓓ our need to eat

Schedules and Forms

Part B

Look at this schedule of library hours. Then answer the questions.

Bayville Library Hours

	Downtown Branch	Maple St. Branch	Lake Branch	Green St. Branch
Monday	9-6	Closed	12-5	10-6
Tuesday	9-6	10-6	10-6	10-6
Wednesday	12-9	10-8	Closed	10-6
Thursday	9-6	10-6	10-6	12-8
Friday	9-5	10-6	10-5	10-6
Saturday	10-6	10-5	10-5	12-5
Sunday	12-6	12-5	12-5	Closed

1. On which day is the Lake branch closed? _____

2. What time does the Downtown branch open on Wednesday? _____

3. What time does the Green Street branch close on Saturday? _____

4. What are the Maple Street branch's Friday hours? _____

Jill Vang wants to get a library card. Use the information on her driver's license to complete the application form.

5–9. Library Card Application

Name: _____
     (first)   (middle)   (last)

Address: _____
      (#)   (street)   (apt. #)

_____
     (city)   (state)   (ZIP code)

Birth date: _____ Gender: F M
     (month)   (day)   (year)

Driver's License #: _____

CALIFORNIA
DRIVER LICENSE
EXPIRES 04-10-05   CA3210777   CLASS C
JILL SHOUA VANG
333 MAIN STREET, APT 1
GILROY, CA 95020
SEX: F   HAIR: BLK
EYES: BRN BIRTH DATE: 06-20-80
HT: 5-06 WT: 130

Part C

Finding Facts on the Internet

Finish these sentences. Tell about two ways you can search for information on the Internet.

1. To go to a Web site, _____

_____

2. To do a key word search, _____

_____

Look at this information from an Internet search engine. Then answer the questions.

Fact **Finder**

Find: | food recipes | SEARCH

Results 1-10 of 563,032 entries found

Grandma's Secret Recipes
...dishes you thought only Grandma could prepare.
Easy-to-follow recipes...

Cookie Classics
...the greatest collection of cookie recipes...Search the
database to find...

---

3. What key words were used to do this search? _____

4. You want some summer recipes. What pair of key words can you add to **food recipes** to help you find what you need?

Ⓐ fun ideas   Ⓒ summer meals

Ⓑ cheap eating   Ⓓ birthday gifts

5. If you want to find information about theme parks in Colorado, what key words would you use? _____ and _____

6. If you want to find information about parks in your city or town, what key words would you use? _____ and _____

TEST TIP

If you are having trouble with a multiple-choice question, first try to eliminate any answers you know are wrong.

Directions and Food Labels

Part D

Read this recipe for hummus (a Middle Eastern bean dip). Then answer the questions that follow.

READING TIP

T is a short way of saying **tablespoon**. A small **t** is short for **teaspoon**.

Hummus

3 cans chick peas (garbanzo beans)
2 cloves garlic (crushed)
1 t salt
2 T tahini (sesame seed paste)

3 T lemon juice
2 T olive oil
1 T fresh parsley

Put the chick peas in a blender. Blend them until they make a paste. Add crushed garlic and salt. Continue blending. Slowly blend in tahini and lemon juice. Add olive oil and blend until creamy. Put the hummus dip in a bowl and sprinkle with parsley. Serve with pita bread.

1. How many cloves of garlic do you need? _____

2. How many cans of chick peas do you use? _____

3–7. Put these steps from the recipe in the right order. Number them 1–5.

____ Slowly blend in tahini and lemon juice.

____ Place hummus in a bowl and sprinkle with parsley.

____ Add crushed garlic and salt and continue blending.

____ Blend the chick peas.

____ Add olive oil and blend until creamy.

SELL BY 02/05

All Natural Ingredients: garbanzo beans, tahini (sesame paste), lemon juice, water, garlic, spices, salt.

HAMMID'S HUMMUS

Look at the labels on the hummus container. Then answer the questions.

Nutrition Facts	Amount/Serving	% DV*	Amount/Serving	% DV*
Serving Size 2 Tbsp. (30g)	**Total Fat** 3.5 g	5%	**Total Carb.** 4g	1%
Servings 8	Sat. Fat 0.5 g	3%	Diet.Fiber 3g	13%
Calories 60	**Cholest.** 0 mg	0%	Sugars 0g	
Fat Calories 40	**Sodium** 120mg	5%	**Protein** 4g	
*Percent Daily Values (DV) are based on a 2,000 calorie diet.	Vitamin A ** • Vitamin C 2%	• Calcium 2%	• Iron 4	

8. Which of these ingredients is in Hammid's Hummus, but NOT in the recipe above?

Ⓐ garbanzo beans

Ⓑ garlic

Ⓒ lemon juice

Ⓓ water

9. What is the last day and month that the store should sell the container of hummus? **month** _____ **year** _____

10. How big is one serving? _____

11. How many calories would you eat if you had three servings?

_____

Introduction

Photographs let you look back into the past. But sometimes, when no words explain what a photo shows, this view can be hazy and confusing.

Study this picture. Then try to answer the questions below.

Who do you think the people in this picture are? Fill in the circle.

Ⓐ cave dwellers from prehistoric times

Ⓑ a Russian dance group

Ⓒ gold miners in the 1850s

Ⓓ a freeway construction crew in the 1960s

What do you think the people are doing?

Ⓐ digging a well

Ⓑ clearing rocks from a mine

Ⓒ lifting up a giant fossil

Ⓓ building an overpass

History Tells the Story

This picture was taken in California in the early 1850s. The people are miners clearing rocks from a gold mine. It would be hard to figure out these facts, unless a book or a caption explained the picture.

History is the study of people, places, and events from the past. Geography is the study of land, water, and other resources. It is also the study of how people have used resources over time. History and geography are connected. For example, if there wasn't gold under the ground, the people in the picture would not have dug a gold mine, and you would not be wondering about this old photo.

Understanding history is an important part of your studies. In Chapter 4 you will learn more about reading and making sense of information about history and geography.

LESSON 23   Previewing and Predicting

Preview, Then Predict

To **preview** a book or passage is to look ahead at it and see what it's about. To **predict** is to guess what a book or passage is about. To preview, follow these steps:

- Read the **title,** the **headings,** and any **subheadings** you find.
- Read the **first sentence** of each paragraph.
- Look at the **pictures** and read the **captions**.

Try It Out

You might find a passage like the one below in a history book.

Follow the steps above to preview it. Then answer these questions.

1. What is the title of the passage? _____

2. What subheading do you see? _____

3. What do you think this passage will mostly be about?

   Ⓐ the town of Coloma   Ⓒ the Gold Rush

   Ⓑ Sutter's Mill   Ⓓ the discovery of gold

Now read the passage.

The California Gold Rush

Gold Discovered at Sutter's Mill In early 1848, James Marshall was building a sawmill for John Sutter. Lumber was badly needed on Sutter's ranch, and the mill was almost finished. Marshall looked down and saw something shiny in the mill's race, or water channel. "I reached my hand down and picked it up," Marshall wrote. "It made my heart thump, for I was certain it was gold. The piece was about half the size and shape of a pea. Then I saw another." He quickly rode to Sutter's ranch house to show him the discovery. Still not quite sure, they tested the nuggets. Yes, they were pure gold. The two men tried to keep it a secret, but word got out quickly.

WORDS TO KNOW

discovered

half

dozens

wealth

supplies

Check Your Prediction

4. Was your prediction correct? ___ yes ___ no

5. Why do you think James Marshall and John Sutter tried to keep the discovery of gold a secret? _____

_____

Make Another Prediction

Preview the next part of the passage below. Then answer these questions.

6. What do you think a **boom time** is?

Ⓐ a slow time

Ⓒ time for a party

Ⓑ a time of fast growth

Ⓓ a loud time

7. Some people made money in other ways besides digging for gold. How do you think they did this?

_____

Now read the passage to see if your predictions were correct.

Boom Times

People left their jobs, families, and hometowns to rush to the gold fields. They were called "49ers" because the first large groups of them came in 1849.

Gold seekers came from near and far, by land and by sea. Mining towns sprang up by the dozens. Within two years, San Francisco alone grew from about 800 people to over 50,000. Some 49ers found gold. Many, however, worked long and hard but did not get rich. Many of those who made the greatest wealth were people who sold supplies, such as shovels, pickaxes, and wheelbarrows, to the miners. One who made a fortune was a man named Levi Strauss. He made a product miners needed badly—sturdy pants made from a thick blue cloth called denim. His pants came to be known as Levi's jeans.

Gold mining was hard, dirty, and often disappointing work.

Check Your Prediction

8. How did some people who never found gold become rich during the California gold rush? _____

_____

LESSON 24   Strategies for Reading History and Geography

SQRR Strategy

How do you make the facts stick when you read a passage about history or geography? This lesson will teach you a strategy for remembering what you read. The strategy is called SQRR. Here is what the letters stand for:

- **S**—**S**urvey, or preview, the passage. Think about what the topic is.
- **Q**—Form a **Q**uestion out of every heading.
- **R**—**R**ead the passage and look for the answers to your questions.
- **R**—**R**ecite the answers, or say them to yourself.

Survey and Question

Survey the passage on the next page. Then answer the questions.

1. What do you think the passage will mostly be about?

   Ⓐ mountains and lowlands   Ⓒ old mountains everywhere

   Ⓑ bodies of water in America   Ⓓ America's waterways and mountains

2. Read the first heading. What would be the best question you could make from this heading?

   Ⓐ Where is the United States?

   Ⓑ What are the major bodies of water in the United States?

   Ⓒ Who needs water?

   Ⓓ What is a landform?

3–4. What facts do you think this passage will include?

facts about mountain ranges: _____

_____

facts about waterways: _____

_____

boundary

range

geologic

basins

plateaus

Read

Now read the passage. Look for the answers to your questions.

Water Systems and Mountains of the United States

Major Bodies of Water The Pacific Ocean forms most of the western coast of the United States. Off the eastern coast lies the Atlantic Ocean. The Gulf of Mexico forms part of the country's southern boundary. The Mississippi, Missouri, and Ohio rivers form the longest river system. The Rio Grande defines part of the United States' southwestern border with Mexico. In the northeast, the St. Lawrence River and Great Lakes define a section of the border with Canada.

Major Mountain Ranges The highest mountain ranges in the United States are in the western half of the country. The Pacific Ranges (Coast Ranges, Cascade Range, and Sierra Nevada) lie near the West Coast. They extend north to south from Alaska to Mexico. East of the Pacific Ranges lie the Rocky Mountains. The Pacific Ranges and the Rocky Mountains are actually part of the same geologic system. They are separated by wide flatlands made of basins and plateaus. The Appalachian Mountains are in the eastern part of the country. In the United States, this range extends from Maine to Alabama.

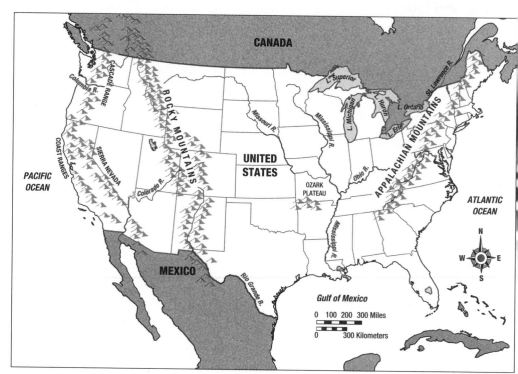

Answer Your Questions

Write answers to the following questions. Use facts from the passage.

5. What are the major bodies of water?

   A off the eastern coast: _____

   B off the western coast: _____

C longest river system: _____

D border with Mexico: _____

E border with Canada: _____

6. What are the major mountain ranges?

A the West Coast: _____

from _____ in the north to _____ in the south

B east of the Pacific Ranges: _____

from _____ in the north to _____ in the south

C the eastern part of the country: _____

from _____ in the north to _____ in the south

Recite

Now look back over the answers to your questions. Say them to yourself over and over, until you know all the facts.

Memory Check

Let's find out if the facts stuck. Finish this crossword puzzle.

Across

3. long river system with the longest name

4. lands between the Pacific Ranges and the Rockies

5. mountains between the Pacific Ranges and the Appalachians

7. coast where the Atlantic is

8. coast where the Pacific is

Down

1. ocean of the West Coast

2. mountains from Maine to Alabama

6. ocean of the East Coast

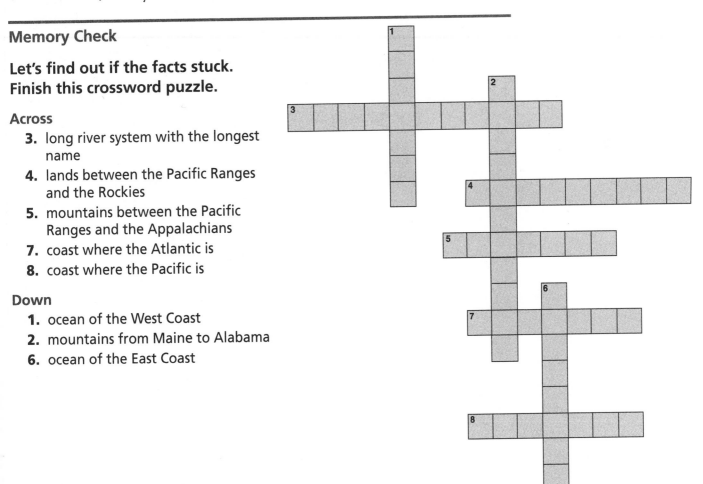

LESSON 25　Finding the Main Idea

Stated Main Ideas

It's hard to remember everything when you read. And really, most of the time you don't need to remember every detail. But it is important to remember the big ideas.

- The **main idea** is the most important idea in a paragraph or passage.
- Many paragraphs have a **main idea sentence** that tells what the paragraph is about.

Read this paragraph. Try to find the main idea.

In 1860 no trains or highways crossed the western United States. (The railroad ended in St. Joseph, Missouri.) Mail delivery depended upon stagecoaches, horse-drawn wagons, boats, or pack mules. It took 30 days for a letter to get from New York to California. First the letter traveled by steamship around the tip of South America to San Francisco. Then it was carried to towns in California by pack mules. Letters could also be sent by overland stagecoach or by wagon train. In 1860, the Central Overland California and Pikes Peak Express Company put together a route of relay stations between St. Joseph, Missouri and Sacramento, California. Riders on galloping horses could travel the route in just 8-10 days. The Pony Express was the fastest way yet of delivering mail quickly across 2,000 miles of the Wild West.

1. What is this paragraph mostly about?

   Ⓐ letters to Missouri　　　Ⓒ the Pony Express

   Ⓑ the Pikes Peak Express　Ⓓ the railroads

2. Which sentence best sums up what the paragraph is about? Reread the paragraph and draw a line under that sentence.

Did you underline the last sentence? Good! That's the main idea sentence. The main idea sentence is often the first or the last sentence in a paragraph.

Details

Details are smaller bits of information that tell more about the main idea. The chart below shows two details from the paragraph.

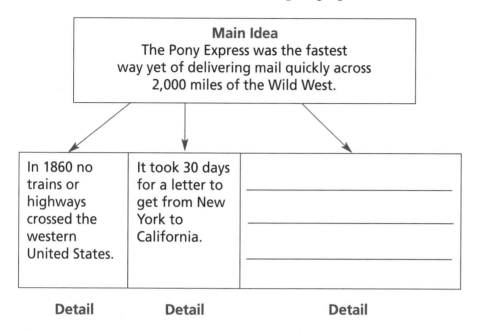

3. Add another detail to the blank box in the chart above.

4. Which of these details could you add to the paragraph?

   Ⓐ The ice cream cone was invented in St. Louis.

   Ⓑ The overland mail route from St. Louis to San Francisco took over three weeks.

   Ⓒ In 1860 most people in the West knew how to ride horses.

   Ⓓ New York was a big city in 1860.

Unstated Main Ideas

Sometimes the main idea is not stated in a sentence. You have to figure it out by adding up the details.

Read this paragraph.

By February of 1860, more than 120 riders, 156 stations, 400 horses, and hundreds of workers were in place along the route. The first rider galloped out of St. Joseph some time after dark on April 3, 1860. The mail was relayed, or handed off, from rider to rider at stations along the route. Riders got fresh horses every 10 or 15 miles. They covered about 10 miles per hour, and rode up to 250 miles a day. New riders took over after a certain distance. Each day, Pony Express riders braved the dangers of riding through wild territory. Most riders were about 20 years old. The youngest rider was only 11. The Pony Express came to an end after 1861. At that time coast-to-coast telegraph service began.

"Wanted: Young, skinny, wiry fellows not over 18. Must be expert riders willing to face death daily. Orphans preferred."

■ What does this ad tell you about the job?

■ Some Pony Express experts think this ad is a fake. What do you think?

WRITING TIP

When you sum up a writer's statement in your own words, try this:

■ Put the words in an order different from the order the writer used.

■ Replace some words with other words that have the same meaning.

5. What is the paragraph on page 81 mostly about?

Ⓐ how the Pony Express worked

Ⓑ how old the riders were

Ⓒ coast-to-coast telegraph service

Ⓓ the 156 Pony Express stations

In the paragraph you read, the main idea is not stated in a sentence. But you can add up the details to figure out the main idea yourself.

Fill in this fact sheet. Look back at the paragraph on page 81 to find the answers.

Pony Express Fact Sheet

6. number of riders needed: _____

7. number of horses needed: _____

8. number of stations: _____

9. how far riders went in a day: _____

10. Which sentence below best sums up these details?

Ⓐ Riders got fresh horses every 12-15 miles.

Ⓑ The Pony Express was a huge undertaking.

Ⓒ The Pony Express ended in 1861.

Ⓓ Pony Express riders got very tired.

Sum It Up

In your own words, tell what the second paragraph on page 81 is about.

11. Main Idea:

_____

_____

12. One Detail:

_____

_____

LESSON 26   Organizing Information Graphically

Some Ideas Are Related

The ideas in nonfiction text are usually tied together. For example, main ideas are related to details because every detail tells more about a main idea. You can show how ideas are related by making an "idea map." There are different kinds of idea maps.

Example

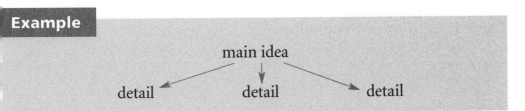

Nonfiction text is usually organized in a way that helps readers understand how ideas are related. The passage at the bottom of this page tells about a **cause** and an **effect**.

- A **cause** is an event that makes another event happen.
- An **effect** is the event that happens as a result.
- Sometimes more than one event happens as a result of a single cause.

Example

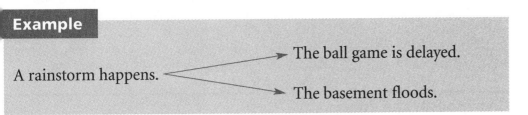

Charting Cause and Effect

Read the passage. Think about the effects of the gold discovery.

A Town Becomes a City

The discovery of gold in California in 1848 had a huge impact on the small town of San Francisco. As word of the discovery spread, people flocked to California from all over the United States. Many people passed through San Francisco on their way to the gold fields. Many also stopped in the city to find fortune in other ways. The city of San Francisco grew almost overnight into a boom town. Ships were abandoned in San Francisco Bay as their owners headed for the gold fields. Business of all kinds sprang up in the city's streets. Banks were needed to handle money. Hardware stores sold supplies. Theaters sprang up to entertain the new crowds. In a very short time, a small town became a thriving city.

WORDS TO KNOW

discovery

impact

fortune

abandoned

thriving

Make a Cause-and-Effect Chart

Write four effects the discovery of gold had on San Francisco.

Effects

1.

2.

Cause

Gold was discovered in California.

Effects

3.

4.

ancient

decomposed

sediment

erosion

Cause and Effect in Geography

The passage below describes one way in which land and landforms change over time.

Read the passage. Look for causes and effects.

The Inland Sea

Long ago, a warm, shallow sea covered much of North America. The bottom of the sea was soft and muddy. When ancient sea creatures died, their bodies sank into the mud. As the creatures decomposed, or rotted away, they became part of the mud and dirt. Over time, layers of sediment made of dead plants and animals built up. Pressure caused the mud to harden into rock.

The inland sea eventually dried up. What had been the sea floor was now dry land. Rivers flowed over the land. The force of rushing water carved valleys in a natural process called erosion. Some valleys became very, very deep. The Grand Canyon, formed by the Colorado River, is more than a mile deep in places. The steep canyon walls tell a geologic story that took millions of years to create.

Chart Causes and Effects

Use details from the passage to complete this cause-and-effect chart.

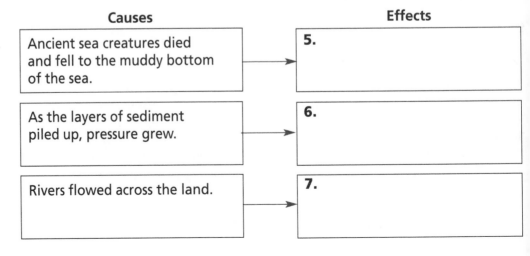

Causes

Causes	Effects
Ancient sea creatures died and fell to the muddy bottom of the sea.	**5.**
As the layers of sediment piled up, pressure grew.	**6.**
Rivers flowed across the land.	**7.**

Charting Sequence of Events

Many passages in history books are organized by **sequence of events**. Some passages in government books list **steps in a process.**

- In a paragraph describing a sequence of events, the events are explained in the order they happened.
- In a paragraph listing steps in a process, steps are given in the order they should be done.
- Sequence words such as **first, next,** and **then** help show the order.

Read the following passage. As you read, think about the order in which the steps happen.

How a Bill Becomes a Law

For an idea to become a law, several steps must take place. First, a member of Congress introduces the idea to Congress. Next, the idea is given a bill number and assigned to a committee within either the Senate or the House of Representatives, depending on where the bill was introduced. The committee studies the bill and decides whether to present it to that house of Congress. If the bill is approved, it gets debated and voted upon. If it passes, the study, debate, and voting steps repeat in the other house of Congress. If the bill passes both houses of Congress, it goes to the President. The President can sign the bill into law or veto it. If the President vetoes the bill, Congress has to pass it again with a two-thirds majority for it to become a law.

Make a Flow Chart

Write the steps for passing a new law in the flow chart below. Write them in the order they happen.

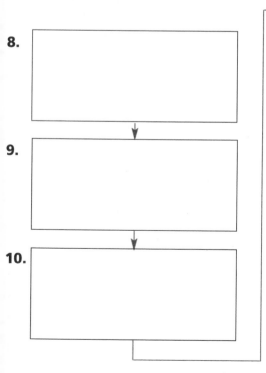

8.

9.

10.

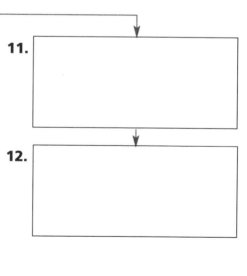

11.

12.

Reading Maps

VOCABULARY BUILDER

The directions **north** and **south** can pair with the directions **east** and **west** to make four new direction words. What are these four directions? (Hint: one is **northeast**.)

Maps

History and geography textbooks include maps to help readers understand where places are located. Most maps show regions, or areas, and the boundaries that separate them. Some maps give other information, such as where resources are located or where people live. Historical maps can help you understand where events took place in the past.

Tips for reading maps:
- Read the **title** of the map to find out what it shows.
- Read the **map key** to find out what the special colors, patterns, or symbols on the map mean.
- Use the **distance scale** to understand how many miles each inch of the map stands for.
- Use the **compass rose** to figure out which direction on the map is north, which is south, which is east, and which is west.

Look at the map below. Then answer the questions.

The United States in 1861

1. What does the map show? _____

2. Look at the map key. What does the thick black line stand for?
   Ⓐ the boundary between the Union and Confederate states
   Ⓑ the boundary between slave states and free states
   Ⓒ the regions that were territories in 1861
   Ⓓ all of the above

3. What is one thing this map helps us understand about the Civil War?
   Ⓐ when the Civil War began and ended
   Ⓑ which states withdrew from the Union
   Ⓒ how many people fought in the Civil War
   Ⓓ which states were free states

4. Which free states were farthest west? (Hint: Use the compass rose to see which direction is west.) _____ and
   _____

Read a Map of Events

The map below shows events as well as places.

Preview the map by reading the title and looking at the map key. Then answer the questions.

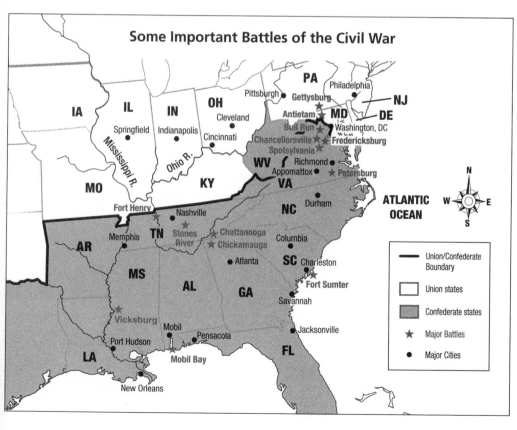

Some Important Battles of the Civil War

Major Civil War Battles	
Fort Sumter	April 12-14, 1861
Bull Run	1st battle: July 21,1861 2nd battle: Aug. 29-30,1862
Fort Henry	Feb. 6, 1862
Antietam	Sept. 17, 1862
Fredericksburg	Dec. 13, 1862
Stones River	Dec. 31, 1862—Jan. 2, 1863
West Virginia	1863
Chancellorsville	May 1-4, 1863
Vicksburg	May 19-July 4, 1863
Gettysburg	July 1-3,1863
Chickamauga	Sept.. 19-20,1863
Chattanooga	Nov. 23-25, 1863
Spotsylvania	May 8-12, 1864
Petersburg	June 20, 1864—April 2, 1865
Mobil Bay	Aug 5, 1864

5. What does the map on page 87 show that the map on page 86 does not show?

Ⓐ the boundary between the Union and Confederate states

Ⓑ how the important battles were won

Ⓒ where and when important battles took place

Ⓓ where state boundaries are located

6. What does the symbol ★ on the map key stand for?

Ⓐ major cities   Ⓒ battle sites

Ⓑ state capitals   Ⓓ port cities

7. What city is nearest to Fort Sumter?

Ⓐ Charleston   Ⓒ Durham

Ⓑ Savannah   Ⓓ Columbia

8. In what year did the battle of Gettysburg take place?

Ⓐ 1861   Ⓒ 1863

Ⓑ 1862   Ⓓ 1864

9. How long did the battle last?

Ⓐ one day   Ⓒ three days

Ⓑ two days   Ⓓ four days

10. Look at the places where most of the battles took place. What conclusion can you draw, based on the locations of the battles?

Ⓐ Most of the fighting happened near the Union-Confederate border.

Ⓑ Most of the fighting happened along the coast.

Ⓒ The Union Army won most of the early battles.

Ⓓ The Confederate Army won most of the early battles.

11. If you wanted to include other information about the Civil War on the map, what symbols would you use for the map key? Draw your ideas in the boxes below.

ships in the harbors	Union victories

LESSON 28   Thinking Critically About Social Studies

Identifying Facts and Opinions

Is every statement you read a fact? No! Many pieces of writing include both facts and opinions. It's important to know the difference between them.

- A **fact** is a statement that can be proven to be true.
  Example of a Fact: Boston is a city in Massachusetts.
- An **opinion** is a statement of belief. You can't prove that an opinion is true.
  Example of an Opinion: Boston is the best city in Massachusetts.

Often what you read about history includes a mix of facts and opinions.

Read these sentences. Write F next to the facts. Write O next to the opinions.

1. _____ In 1773, America was an English colony.

2. _____ The British made laws the colonists had to obey.

3. _____ The laws the British passed were very unfair.

4. _____ The colonists should have refused to obey them.

5. _____ Boston was an established city in colonial times.

6. _____ Boston Harbor was a great spot for eating lunch.

Look for Opinions

Read the paragraph below.

7–16. Draw a line under each sentence that is a fact. Circle each sentence that is an opinion.

The Boston Tea Party was one of the bravest actions of the American colonists. The British Parliament had placed a tax on tea. Many colonists hated this tax. They felt this way because the colonists were given no say about the tax and they believed this was unfair. In late 1773, three British ships loaded with tea sailed into Boston Harbor. A group of colonists wanted to protest the tea tax, so one night they dressed up as Native Americans. They snuck onto the ships and broke open all the tea chests. They threw about 90,000 pounds of tea into the harbor. The colonists were well-behaved during the event. They did not damage the ship or any of the other cargo.

WORDS TO KNOW

colony

colonists

British Parliament

cargo

READING TIP

Some words are clues that a statement is an opinion. Words like **best, worst, bravest,** and **greatest** all show that a judgment is being made. A judgment is one kind of opinion.

Answer these questions about the passage.

17. Why is the first sentence you circled an opinion and not a fact?

   Ⓐ Everyone knows that the Boston Tea Party never really happened.

   Ⓑ No one can prove that this protest was the bravest act the colonists ever did.

   Ⓒ No one can prove that there was tea on the ship.

   Ⓓ The Boston Tea Party did not require bravery.

18. Why is the second sentence you circled an opinion and not a fact?

   Ⓐ People have different ideas about what it means to be "well-behaved."

   Ⓑ There were no well-behaved people in the colonies.

   Ⓒ No one can prove that the colonists really dumped the tea.

   Ⓓ It's not possible for anyone to have this opinion.

19–21. Reread the third sentence. ("Many colonists hated this tax.") Check the three things you could do to prove that this sentence is a fact.

   ____ Read an encyclopedia article about the Boston Tea Party.

   ____ Read letters or newspaper articles written in Boston in 1773.

   ____ Think about how you would feel if you were a colonist.

   ____ Ask an expert about the American Revolution how colonists felt about the tax.

Recognizing Bias

Being able to spot opinions will help you be a more critical reader. Being able to spot **bias** is also important.

- **Bias** is a strong personal feeling for or against something.
- If a writer is **biased,** he or she may not present information fairly.
- A biased writer might use "loaded language" to give readers a certain feeling about a topic. For example, the words **shameful** and **cowardly** can affect how a reader thinks about a person or an action.
- A biased writer might present only one side of an issue, or leave out facts that don't support his or her personal view.

Imagine that the following newspaper article appeared in a Boston newspaper the day after the Boston Tea Party. Read the article. Ask yourself if the author is biased, and if so, how.

Cowardly Colonists Waste Good Tea

Last night a gang of colonists dressed up in costumes and invaded Boston harbor. They boarded three British ships. They then broke into the tea chests and dumped many pounds of choice tea into the bay!

Local residents were shocked when they heard about the cowardly tea-dumping. "It's a shame," said one shopkeeper. "There's no excuse for wasting good tea!"

"This really worries me," said another shopkeeper. "It doesn't make us colonists look very good, does it?"

People are saying that the tea-dumping was a protest against the new tax on tea. Some hotheads may object to the tax, but reasonable citizens understand that the new tax is necessary and fair. We all must hope that the criminals who committed this shameful act will be caught and punished in a fitting manner.

Answer these questions about the article.

22. Whose side do you think the writer of this article is on?

(A) the colonists

(B) the British

(C) the Native Americans

(D) He is not taking sides.

23. What important fact did the writer leave out?

(A) The colonists dumped 90,000 pounds of tea.

(B) King George lived in England, not America.

(C) It was hard work to dump that much tea in the harbor.

(D) Many colonists hated the tea tax.

24. Think about the quotes the writer included from the people of Boston. Why do you think he chose to include these quotes?

(A) They support his own view of the event.

(B) They express both sides.

(C) They support the colonists' view.

(D) They are the only ones he could find.

25. Which phrase is an example of "loaded language"?

(A) dressed up in costumes

(B) shameful act

(C) local residents

(D) a protest against the new tax

Part A

Previewing and Predicting; SQRR

- To **preview** a passage is to look at it before reading to see what it is about.

- To **predict** is to make a guess about a passage, based on the preview.

Preview the passage that follows. Then answer the questions.

1. What do you think the passage will mostly be about?

   Ⓐ women as entertainers

   Ⓑ a population out of balance

   Ⓒ a woman named Lotta Crabtree

   Ⓓ women during the Gold Rush

2. What main point do you think the passage will make?

   Ⓐ Women were scarce in the gold mining towns.

   Ⓑ Grizzly bears and monkeys were popular pets.

   Ⓒ Women could pan for gold as well as men could.

   Ⓓ Everything was out of balance during the Gold Rush.

3–5. What questions could you make out of the three subheadings?

   A. _____

   B. _____

   C. _____

Now read the passage. Look for the answers to your questions.

Women in the Gold Rush

A Population Out of Balance Most of the people who rushed to California to search for gold were men. A few of the gold seekers were accompanied by their wives, but women were very scarce. Because women were scarce, the appearance of a woman in a small town or mining camp was often a big event.

A New World of Possibilities The women who did move to California found that their skills were very much in demand. Few men could cook or sew. The gold towns were filled with hungry miners whose clothes needed mending. Quite a few women began successful businesses by meeting these needs. Some started laundries or sewing shops. Others ran boardinghouses where weary travelers could get a hot meal.

Women Entertainers in the Gold Towns Gold miners lived a hard and dangerous life. They had few comforts, and they were far from home. Entertainment, when they could find it, was highly prized. One favorite of the miners was Lotta Crabtree, a very young performer who traveled through the gold towns for several years. She danced and sang, and the miners loved her. Later she moved to San Francisco and then to New York. In time she became the highest paid actress in the United States.

Lotta Crabtree gave her first public performance at the age of seven.

6–8. Write the answers to your questions on the lines.

A. _____

B. _____

C. _____

9. Were your predictions about the passage correct? ___ yes ___ no

10. Why do you think Lotta Crabtree was so popular with the miners?

_____

_____

Organizing Information Graphically   Part B

Use the information from the passage to complete the items below.

1–3. Finish the main idea and detail chart below.

> **main idea:** California offered women a lot of possibilities.

detail:_____

_____

_____

_____

detail:_____

_____

_____

_____

detail:_____

_____

_____

_____

4–5. Finish the cause-effect chart below.

cause:
Most gold seekers were men.

effect: _____

_____

effect: _____

_____

6–9. Finish the flow chart below. Write the main events in Lotta Crabtree's life.

Lotta Crabtree began her career
_____

Then she moved to
_____

She moved to
_____

She later became
_____

Part C   Reading Maps

Use the map below to answer the questions.

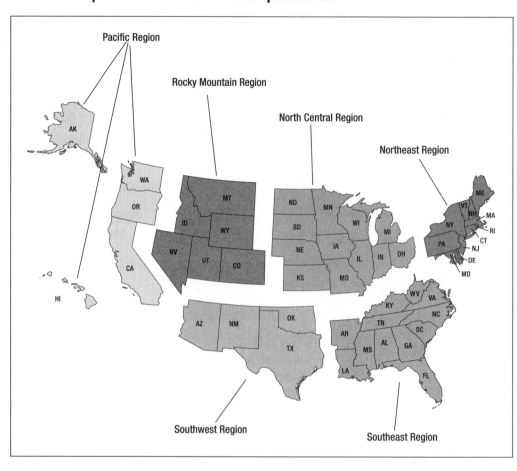

1. What special information does this map show?
   Ⓐ the regions of the United States
   Ⓑ the boundaries between countries
   Ⓒ the rivers of the United States
   Ⓓ a compass rose and map key

2. Which region shown on the map is farthest east?

   _____

3. Which region shown on the map is farthest west?

   _____

4. Find your state on the map. What region is it in?

   _____

Thinking Critically: Facts, Opinions, and Bias

Part D

Read the passage. Then answer the questions.

Little Lotta Crabtree performed a song and dance act on Saturday night at the Grass Valley Theater. Some say that hardworking miners need a bit of entertainment to keep their spirits up. While that may be true, it is a cruel act to make a young child perform on the stage of a rough mining town.

Lotta grew up in Grass Valley. It's true that she knew most of the people in the audience. Even so, the lights and noise must have frightened her. What decent mother would allow a child to spend time with singers, dancers, and other loose theater people? The citizens of Grass Valley should be ashamed that one of their own sweet children is being forced into such a situation.

1. Do you think the author of this article has a bias? If so, what is the article for or against?

   _____

   _____

2–7. Write **F** next to each statement that is a fact. Write **O** next to each statement that is an opinion.

   ___ Lotta performed a song and dance act.

   ___ Miners need entertainment.

   ___ Lotta grew up in Grass Valley.

   ___ It is wrong to have a child perform on a stage.

   ___ Lotta knew most of the people in the audience.

   ___ The people of Grass Valley should be ashamed.

8. Which phrase is an example of loaded language?

   Ⓐ loose theater people   Ⓒ citizens of Grass Valley

   Ⓑ hardworking miners   Ⓓ young child

9. Which fact should the author have included to give a fair description of Lotta?

   Ⓐ Lotta looks young for her age.

   Ⓑ There isn't a lot to do in Grass Valley.

   Ⓒ Grass Valley is an important mining town.

   Ⓓ Lotta loves performing, and her family supports her.

- A **fact** is a statement that can be proved.

- An **opinion** is a statement of belief. It cannot be proved.

- **Bias** is a strong personal feeling for or against something. A writer who is biased may not present information fairly.

TEST TIP

When answering a true-false question, first decide which answer choices are obviously false. Then think about the remaining choices.

Introduction

Every day scientists around the world are working to unlock mysteries and solve problems. Some are trying to find out what causes diseases. Others are exploring the vast frontier of space. Still others are working hard to improve the products we use in daily life.

Knowing how to read science material helps you do well in school. It also helps you stay in touch with important changes in the world of science as they happen. Chapter 5 is about reading and making sense of information about science.

Take a Science Quiz
Try your hand at answering these questions.

Where do comets come from?

    Ⓐ the inside of a star

    Ⓑ "comet zones" in space

    Ⓒ a comet factory

    Ⓓ the earth's atmosphere

What is a tsunami?

    Ⓐ a giant wave

    Ⓑ a Japanese snack

    Ⓒ a volcanic eruption

    Ⓓ a tropical fish

If an animal were cloned, what would the result be?

    Ⓐ It would be twice as tall.

    Ⓑ There would two of it.

    Ⓒ It would disappear.

    Ⓓ It would stay young forever.

Can people make plastic products from plants?

    ___ yes   ___ no

You'll find the answers to these and other questions as you read Chapter 5.

Word Roots: Cracking the Science Code
Articles about science often contain long words that sound complicated. Many science words come from Greek or Latin roots. Knowing some roots and their meanings can help you figure out many words that have to do with science. Read these roots and their meanings:

    sol—"sun"   **orbis**—"circle"   **ast**—"star"

Write each word from the box next to its meaning. Use the word roots to help you.

orbit	astronomer	solar

"having to do with the sun" _____

"one who studies stars" _____

"a circular path" _____

LESSON 29   Previewing and Predicting

Make a Prediction

Preview the passage on this page and the next page by reading the title, headings, and captions. Then answer these questions.

WORDS TO KNOW

comet

solar system

oblong

orbit

nucleus

1. What information do you think this passage will present? Put a check next to your answers.

_____ what makes up a comet

_____ the planets in our solar system

_____ where comets come from

_____ careers in comet-watching

2. Reread the caption that goes with the photo of Halley's Comet. What can you predict you'll learn about comets, based on the caption?

Ⓐ Poorly constructed comets crash into the earth.

Ⓑ The most famous comets are visible all the time.

Ⓒ Comets follow an oval-shaped path, coming in and out of our view.

Ⓓ The last time Halley's Comet will ever be visible is 2062.

Now read the passage.

Comets

A comet is a body of dust and frozen gases, something like a large, dirty snowball. Comets move in huge, oblong orbits around the sun. Most of the time they are too far away to be seen. When they come near the sun, they may be seen from Earth for a few days to a few months.

Parts of a Comet When far from the sun, comets are dense and solid. They may be a few miles across in diameter. As the comet nears the sun, gases and dust stream off the nucleus of the comet. The dust forms a huge cloud around the comet. Light from the sun bounces off the dust and gases, making the comet shine brightly. Part of the cloud trails behind, forming a tail up to 100 million miles long. The tail always extends in the direction away from the sun.

Where Comets Come From Astronomists believe that comets originate in two areas outside our solar system. Some comets come from an area called the Kuiper belt, which has about 200,000 comets. The Oort belt is another huge storage area of comets. This area is thought to have more than 100 billion comets.

Some Famous Comets

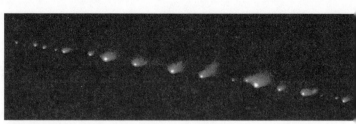

Shoemaker-Levy 9 passed so close to Jupiter in 1992 that it broke into fragments. The pieces crashed into Jupiter in 1994 as the comet made its return trip away from the sun.

Hale-Bopp *(1997), left, was larger than most. Its nucleus may be 19 to 25 miles across.*

Halley's Comet, *above, orbits the sun once every 76 years. It last appeared in 1986 and is next due in 2062.*

Check Your Predictions

3. Were your predictions about the passage correct? ____ yes ____ no

4. Why can't we see a particular comet all the time?

_____

_____

Word Roots: Cracking the Science Code

5. The word **nucleus** has the Latin root word **nux**, which means "kernel or nut." What can you figure out about the nucleus of a comet, based on the meaning of the root?

   Ⓐ The nucleus forms the comet's outer wall.

   Ⓑ The nucleus is the size of a nut.

   Ⓒ The nucleus is the solid part of a comet.

   Ⓓ Comets are goofy.

6. The Latin root **orig** means "beginning." **To originate** means what?

   Ⓐ to get past   Ⓒ to appear

   Ⓑ to be stored   Ⓓ to start

7–8. What other words probably share the **orig** root? Mark two.

   Ⓐ origin   Ⓒ original

   Ⓑ orange   Ⓓ organize

LESSON 30   Strategies for Reading Science

Taking Notes

In Chapter 2 you learned that taking notes is a good way of remembering what you read. Taking notes is especially useful when reading about science.

Note-Taking Review

- When you take notes, jot down the most important ideas and details, including important science words.
- Write in short phrases that are easy to remember.
- After you have finished taking notes, reread the passage. Make sure you didn't leave out an important fact.

Preview and Predict

Preview the passage that follows, and think about what information it will present. Then read the passage. As you read, underline important words and ideas.

Tsunamis

A Different Kind of Wave Tsunamis are powerful ocean waves that sometimes crash onto shore and cause great damage. The word **tsunami** comes from two Japanese words: **tsu** for harbor, and **nami** for wave. Tsunamis take place when underwater landslides, earthquakes, volcanoes, or falling meteorites cause a sudden change in the height of a column of ocean water. Underwater volcanic eruptions or landslides cause a column of water to lift up, then drop, as the water seeks to level out. On the other hand, falling meteorites cause the water level to drop first. Undersea earthquakes can cause the water to drop or rise, but the effect is the same. A set of powerful waves spreads out from that place.

A Deadly Wall of Water Tsunami waves become dangerous only when they reach the coast. Out in the open sea, tsunamis can be hard to spot. In deep waters, tsunamis travel at speeds of up to 600 miles per hour. The waves may be only about 3 feet in height, and up to 1 hour, or 60 miles, apart. A ship may not even notice a tsunami passing under it. As a tsunami moves into shallower areas near the coast, it is slowed down and pushed upward. By the time a tsunami crashes onto shore, it can be up to 100 feet high.

WORDS TO KNOW

tsunami

damage

volcanoes

meteorites

column

READING TIP

If you're unsure of how to pronounce a word, look up the word in a dictionary. Read the respelling.

Finish these notes by writing facts from the passage on page 101 on the lines.

1. paragraph 1: What are tsunamis?

• What they are:_____

_____

• Where they happen: _____

_____

_____

• What can cause them:_____

1._____

2._____

3._____

4._____

2. paragraph 2: Are tsunamis dangerous?

• What happens in the open sea: _____

_____

_____

1. How fast: _____

2. How high: _____

3. How far apart: _____

• What happens in shallow water near the coast:

_____

_____

_____

Practice Taking Notes

Read the last part of the passage below. Then take notes about it on the card that follows.

Predicting Tsunamis Tsunamis are hard to predict because they are barely visible as they travel across the ocean. However, the ability to predict these killer waves would save thousands of lives. Most tsunamis are caused by earthquakes on the floor of the Pacific Ocean. One of the best ways to predict them is to detect such earthquakes using a seismograph (or earthquake measuring) network. Another way to predict tsunamis is to use special tools that detect swells in the deep ocean. Satellites are also used to measure sudden changes in sea level. The Tsunami Warning System in the Pacific Ocean tries to predict where and when tsunamis will hit, and warns people to move to higher ground.

3. paragraph 3: _____

_____?

(answers this question)

_____

_____

_____

_____

_____

_____

_____

_____

Word Roots: Cracking the Science Code

The Greek root **seismos** (sīz′ mōs) means "earthquake." The Greek root **graph** means "write." The ending **ist** means "one who practices." The ending **ology** means "the study of." Write each word in the box next to its meaning. Use the roots and endings to help you.

seismograph	seismologist	seismology

4. the study of earthquakes _____

5. a person who studies earthquakes _____

6. a machine that records how strong earthquakes are _____

Remembering What You Read

Summarizing

You have already learned some good ways to make information you read stick with you:

- You can use the SQRR strategy to Survey, Question, Read, and Recite key facts.
- You can take notes as you read.
- You can reread material, ask yourself questions about it, and share the facts you learn with a friend.

Another good way to remember what you read is to summarize, or sum up, the most important ideas and details.

- A **summary** is a short restatement of main ideas and important details.
- A summary is written in **your own words**.
- A summary is **much shorter** than the original passage.
- A summary does not contain opinions.

Read the first part of the passage below. Think about what should go into a summary of it.

WORDS TO KNOW

fossil fuels

polymers

molecules

protein

bacteria

biotechnology

Eat the Cup, Too? Plastics Made from Plants

The Problem with Plastics Since the 1950s, plastics have been used to make many things used in daily life. Food containers, pipes, paints, trash bags, bottles, shoes, computers, and many other useful things are made from plastic. One problem with used plastic is that it does not decompose, or break down, easily or quickly. Once it is thrown away, it may sit in landfills for hundreds of years. Another problem is that many plastics are made from fossil fuels such as oil and gas. These fuels are not cheap to find, and our earth has only a limited supply of them.

1–2. Which two sentences below belong in a summary of this paragraph? Check them.

_____ Plastic is used to make a great variety of products.

_____ We use plastic food containers.

_____ Because plastic doesn't easily decompose, it sits in landfills for hundreds of years.

3–4. What other important ideas should the summary include? Check two.

_____ Plastics are made from fossil fuels, which are expensive and in limited supply.

_____ Despite the usefulness of plastic, the material poses problems.

_____ Oil and gas are fossil fuels.

Write a Summary

5–10. Now write your own summary of the paragraph about plastics on page 102. Use important ideas you checked above, but restate these ideas in your own words.

_____

_____

_____

_____

_____

_____

Do It Yourself

Read the rest of the passage.

A Solution: Bio-Polymers Plastics are one kind of polymer. Polymers are huge molecules. They are made up of long chains or networks of smaller molecules. Plants make natural polymers, including starches and proteins, that break down in nature. Scientists are now discovering ways to make useful plastic polymers from living things such as plants and microorganisms such as bacteria. This new kind of science is called **biotechnology**.

Plastic containers, film, bowls, plates, drinking cups, and egg cartons can now be made from starch polymers. The polymers used to make these products come from sugar, barley, corn, rice, soy, or wheat plants. Microorganisms such as bacteria are added to a liquid mix of plant matter, such as a big vat of sugar cane. The microorganisms react with the sugar and starches to make polymers. The result is plastic made from plants. After the plastic product is used, it can be eaten, fed to animals, or dissolved in water. Or it can be put in a compost pile, where it will break down quickly.

Sum It Up

11–14. Put a check next to four ideas you would include in a summary of the second part of the passage.

_____ Plastics are one kind of polymer.

_____ Scientists can now make plastic polymers from plants.

_____ Plastics made from plants can be dissolved in water.

_____ Wheat, barley, corn, and sugar cane contain sugar.

_____ An edible plastic cup probably wouldn't taste very good.

_____ When bacteria is added to plant matter, it can break down the plants into a substance that is like plastic.

_____ Unlike plastics made from fossil fuels, plastics from plants break down easily.

15. One of the sentences above is an opinion, not a fact. Put an X in front of it.

16. One fact above was not in the passage. Cross it out.

17–21. Now write a summary of the second part of the passage on page 103. Remember to restate the sentences in your own words.

_____

_____

_____

_____

_____

_____

WRITING TIP

When you summarize, restate sentences in your own words.

■ Change the order of the words in the original sentence.

■ Replace some words with synonyms that have the same meaning.

Word Roots: Cracking the Science Code

22. An **organism** is a living thing. **Mikros** is a Greek root meaning "small." What is a **microorganism**?_____

_____

23. The word **technology** refers to the skillful use of tools to make things. The root **bio** means "life." What do you think **biotechnology** is?

_____

_____

LESSON 32   Understanding Technical Terms

Word Attack Strategies

Science writing often contains technical words that may be new to you. You've learned that word roots can help you figure out some words. You can also use other strategies.

- Use **context clues** to help you figure out word meaning.
- Use your knowledge of **letter sounds** to figure out how to say words.
- Look for **smaller words** you know inside longer words.
- Think about **related words,** or words you've already learned that may be used in new ways.
- If all else fails, use a **dictionary** or ask a **friend.**

Read this passage. Think about the meaning of the words in dark type.

How CDs and DVDs Are Made

Plastic CDs or DVDs sold at stores are made from master disks. The **mastering** process takes place in several steps. The first master disk, called a "mother," is made of glass coated with a **liquid polymer**. Next, the data (or information) must be **encoded** onto the mother. The data might be sound or music, photographs or text, video, or computer programs. The data has to be **converted** into a **digital** code. That is, it must be broken down into millions of bits of code using only the numbers 0 and 1. A **laser,** or strongly focused light beam, "burns" or "writes" these codes onto the polymer layer. The "writing" is a series of pits and non-pits, called lands, along a **spiral** track. The track begins near the center of the disk and spirals outward.

Next, a thin disk of nickel metal is pressed against the mother, making a perfect metal copy of the track. This copy is called a stamper or "father." The final plastic copies of the disk are made from the father. Hot, melted plastic is stamped, then cooled. The cooled plastic layer is covered with a shiny, **reflective** metal layer. Finally, a protective coating of clear **lacquer** covers the two lower layers. The **transparent** layer allows a laser inside a CD or DVD player to read the encoded track. The metal layer helps reflect the light beam. After a label is printed on it, the disk is then packaged and sold.

THINK ABOUT IT

Technology moves so fast that what is new today may be outdated tomorrow. Do you think it is wiser for consumers to buy new technology products as they are invented, or wait until those products become cheaper and better? Why?

Think About Words

Use word attack strategies to find the meaning of each word below. A suggested strategy for each word is given on the right.

Try this Word Attack Strategy...

1. The base word of **mastering** is _____.

  Ⓐ mast

  Ⓑ master

  Ⓒ mastermind

  Ⓓ aster

Reread the first sentence from the passage on page 105. Look for a shorter form of **mastering**.

2. In this context, **master** means _____.

  Ⓐ to become expert at

  Ⓑ original, or first-made

  Ⓒ mister

  Ⓓ boss or supervisor

Reread the first two sentences. Look for context clues.

3. A **liquid polymer** is _____.

  Ⓐ a many-sided shape

  Ⓑ a liquid made of bacteria

  Ⓒ a biotechnical soft drink

  Ⓓ plastic that can be poured

You learned the word **polymer** in Lesson 31. It's what plastics are made of. What is a **liquid** polymer?

4. A synonym for **data** is _____.

  Ⓐ information

  Ⓑ baby talk for "daddy"

  Ⓒ a mastering process

  Ⓓ a date

Reread the sentence **data** first appears in. It tells the meaning of this word by giving a synonym.

5. **Encoded** means _____.

  Ⓐ came to an end

  Ⓑ entered into a code book

  Ⓒ changed into code

  Ⓓ cooled by a laser

Remove the prefix **en** and the final **d**. Find the base word, **code**. Then read the rest of the paragraph. It tells what **encoded** means.

6. **Converted** means _____.

  Ⓐ changed

  Ⓑ confused

  Ⓒ contacted

  Ⓓ cornered

You may have seen other forms of this word, such as **convert** ("to change into a new form") and **conversion** ("the new form of something").

7. How many syllables does **digital** have?

Ⓐ one

Ⓑ two

Ⓒ three

Ⓓ our

Every syllable has at least one vowel sound. How many vowel sounds do you hear in **digital**?

8. Reflective material _____.

Ⓐ reacts quickly to heat

Ⓑ has a dull surface

Ⓒ is related to other materials

Ⓓ bends or throws back light that shines on it

Remove the ending **ive** and find the base word. A mirror and a piece of glass **reflect** light and other images. What does **reflective** material do?

9. What does the word **lacquer** rhyme with?

Ⓐ quacking

Ⓑ cracker

Ⓒ hanker

Ⓓ quartz

This word has an unusual consonant pattern in the middle. The dictionary respelling can help you figure out how to say it: **lak´ər.**

10. A **transparent** substance is one you can _____.

Ⓐ change easily

Ⓑ find the parents of

Ⓒ make bigger

Ⓓ see through

Trans is a Latin root that means "across." **Apparere** is a Latin verb that means "to show," as in the word **appear** ("to come into view").

Word Roots: Cracking the Science Code

Read each root and its meaning. Then find three words from the box below that share this root. Write the words on the lines.

aud = to hear	**graph** = to write	**scop** = to see
11. _____	14. _____	17. _____
12. _____	15. _____	18. _____
13. _____	16. _____	19. _____

graphite	audio	telescope
microscopic	pentagraph	auditorium
graphic	auditory	scope

LESSON 33   Understanding Graphs and Other Visuals

Chapters in science books often include diagrams, graphs, charts, and other visual aids. Knowing how to read and think about information given visually will help you understand science concepts.

Cutaway Diagrams

A diagram is a picture that shows the different parts of something. Diagrams often have labels with lines that point to the parts of the picture they tell about. A **cutaway** diagram is a picture that lets viewers see both the surface and the inside of something.

Study this cutaway diagram. Then fill in the correct circle.

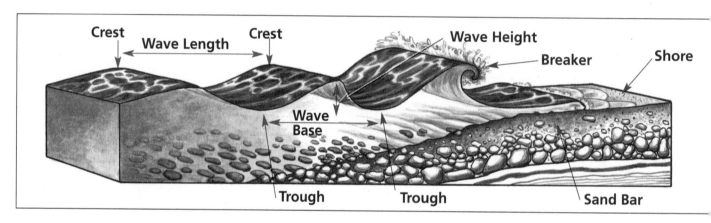

1. What does the diagram show?

   Ⓐ how deep the ocean is

   Ⓑ the cause of a tsunami

   Ⓒ how a wave breaks near the shore

   Ⓓ a tsunami warning system

2. What is the highest part of an ocean wave called?

   Ⓐ the trough

   Ⓑ the crest

   Ⓒ the breaker

   Ⓓ the wave length

3. When does the wave gain height and form a **breaker**?

   Ⓐ when it comes to a shallow area near the shore

   Ⓑ when it rolls back toward the sea

   Ⓒ when it forms a crest in the ocean

   Ⓓ when it comes out of the trough

4. A **wave length** is _____.

   Ⓐ the distance from the base to the height of a wave

   Ⓑ the time it takes a wave to form a breaker

   Ⓒ the distance between the trough and the crest

   Ⓓ the distance from one wave's crest to the next

Bar Graphs

A **bar graph** is a chart that shows numbers or amounts. To read a bar graph, read the title and the information at the top or bottom of the graph. Also read the information on its side. The words tell what the graph is showing. The numbers tell the quantities shown. Then look at the height of each bar.

Study the graph below. Then answer the questions.

5. What do the bars show?

Ⓐ how high some tsunamis were, in meters

Ⓑ how long it took some tsunamis to reach shore

Ⓒ where and when each tsunami occurred

Ⓓ how much damage each tsunami caused, in millions of dollars

6. Where and when did the biggest tsunami in the graph hit shore?

place   year

7. Tsunamis do not reach a height of exactly 5, 10, 15, 20, 25, 30, or 35 meters. Most of the waves in this graph reached an odd height between these numbers. About how high was the wave that hit Indonesia in 1994?

Ⓐ a little less than 20m—about 19m

Ⓑ a little less than 15m—about 14m

Ⓒ a little less than 30m—about 29m

Ⓓ in between 10 and 15m—about 12.5m

8. Add a tsunami to the graph. Write **Philippines, 1994** in the space where it would go. Color the bar so it shows a height of 10 meters.

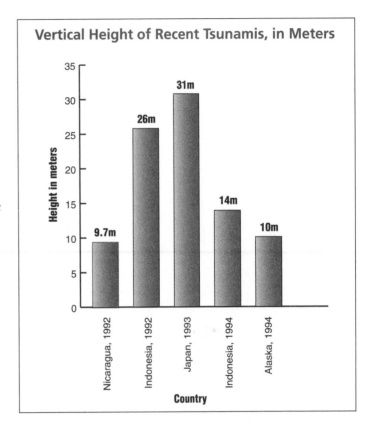

Vertical Height of Recent Tsunamis, in Meters

Symbols

Symbols are pictures that stand for ideas. Scientists use symbols to stand for chemicals, quantities, and many other things. The chart below shows international weather symbols.

Use the symbols to answer the questions.

International Weather Symbols

◯	clear sky	••	steady rain
◗	cloudy sky	•	on-and-off rain
◔	very cloudy sky	Γ	thunderstorm
✳✳	steady snow	ß	heavy thunderstorm
✳	on-and-off snow	S	sandstorm

9. What does this forecast mean?   ◗   •   ••

_____, then _____, followed by _____

10. If you saw this symbol, what would you need?   ✳✳

   Ⓐ sunscreen   Ⓒ a lightning rod

   Ⓑ warm clothes and a hat   Ⓓ an umbrella

11. What is the difference between these two weather events?

   Γ   ß   The first one means _____, and
                 the second one means _____.

12–14. It's your turn to make the forecast. In the boxes, draw the symbols for this sequence: clear skies, followed by on-and-off snow, then steady snow.

LESSON 34   Thinking Critically About Science

What Do You Think?

Advances in science give us the ability to do many things we were once unable to do, such as:

- predict tsunamis
- study comets millions of miles away
- store music, photos, and movies on CDs and DVDs

People don't always agree about whether innovations like these are good. Some people ask, "Should we do things just because we can?" People also disagree about the best way to spend money on scientific research. They ask questions like, "Should the government spend billions of dollars on exploring space? Why not spend that money on curing cancer or stopping hunger?"

People who ask questions like these are **thinking critically** about science. To think critically is to think carefully about issues and what they mean. It means making judgments about what is and isn't right or important.

Decide how important each of the following advancements is. Write a number from 1 (most important) to 4 (least important) next to each item below.

_____ predicting tsunamis

_____ studying comets

_____ making plastic from plants

_____ storing data on CDs

On the lines below, tell why you rated the most important advance as you did.

#1: _____ Why: _____

_____

_____

Tell why you rated the least important advance from page 111 as you did.

#4: _____ Why: _____

_____

_____

WORDS TO KNOW

clone

nucleus

individual

genetic

controversy

Consider Both Sides

The next passage describes an issue many people disagree about—cloning.

Read the passage. Think about what is good and not good about cloning.

Should Human Cloning Take Place?

A clone is an exact copy of a living being. Clones are made by fusing the nucleus of an female egg cell to a living cell of another individual. The fusing is done with electricity. This makes a new cell. A new individual can grow from the new cell. The new individual has the exact genetic traits of the individual who gave the cell. Another form of cloning creates cells and tissues that could help repair diseased human tissues or organs. In the 1990s, scientists cloned mice, cows, and sheep.

The idea of cloning causes great controversy. Some people believe cloning is the best hope to cure many diseases. On the other hand, many people believe that cloning is dangerous and wrong. Many who are against cloning argue that most cloning efforts end in failure. It took 277 tries to clone Dolly the sheep! Animal clones usually do not survive until birth. Those that do survive often have deformed organs or body parts, or weak health. Others believe it is wrong to change the course of nature to such an extent. They argue that cloning may have far-reaching effects no one has thought about.

Think About It

What is your first response, based on the information in the passage?

1. Animals _____ be cloned.
        (should/should not)

Think Deeper

People have put forth many reasons for why cloning should and should not be done.

The situations described below argue in favor of cloning. Next to each one, write a plus sign or a minus sign to show if you agree or disagree.

+ = Cloning would be OK for this purpose.

− = Cloning would not be OK for this purpose.

+ or −

2. Cloning cattle and sheep could result in higher quality animal products, such as meat and wool. _____

3. Some animals exhibit traits such as high intelligence. Cloning them could result in a smarter breed of animals, better able to help humans. An example is dogs who assist blind people. _____

4. Cloning animal tissues could provide cures for many diseases animals now suffer from. _____

Write About It

5–10. On the lines below, write a paragraph giving your opinion about whether animals should be cloned. Give at least two reasons why you think as you do.

_____

_____

_____

_____

_____

_____

Part A

Previewing and Predicting; Taking Notes

- To preview a passage is to read the title, headings, and captions to see what it is about.

- To predict is to guess what information will be presented, based on the preview.

- To take notes is to jot down the most important ideas and details, as an aid to remembering what you read.

Preview the following passage and answer the questions below. Then read the passage to see if your predictions were correct.

1. What do you think the passage will be about?

   _____

   _____

2. Based on the subheadings, what do you think is true of tsunamis?
   - Ⓐ Tsunamis are easy to spot from land.
   - Ⓑ A tsunami wave hits all at once.
   - Ⓒ People can avoid tsunamis, if they are careful.
   - Ⓓ A tsunami can consist of several waves.

Strike Without Warning

A Tsunami Approaches Deep at sea, a giant wave makes its way toward shore. The wave travels at about 450 miles per hour, but the ships it quietly rolls beneath do not even notice it. As the wave nears land, it begins to change. It loses speed, but it grows taller.

The First Signs To a person on the shore, the approaching tsunami doesn't look like much. It may look like the swelling of a high tide. However, if the land near the shore is especially shallow, the tsunami may reach a height of several meters. The swell first might be followed by a sudden onrush of water—much larger than the path of an ordinary wave as it rushes onto shore.

A Deadly Set of Waves As the water from this first swell rushes back into the sea, its force may strip the beach of rocks and driftwood. The true destruction, though, is yet to come. After several minutes, the first monster wave hits the shore. It sweeps across the beach and rushes inland to flood the coast. Several more giant waves follow. In general, the crests of the third to eighth waves are the largest and most destructive.

Check Your Predictions

3–4. In general, what is true of tsunamis? Fill in two circles.
   - Ⓐ A tsunami can strike as a series of waves.
   - Ⓑ Not more than two waves make up a tsunami.
   - Ⓒ You can best feel a tsunami in the open ocean.
   - Ⓓ The third to eighth waves are highest.

Take Notes

In the space below, take notes about the first two paragraphs of the passage from page 114. Remember to use short phrases instead of complete sentences (5–8).

Paragraph 1: _____

_____

_____

_____

Paragraph 2: _____

_____

_____

_____

TEST TIP

When completing multiple-choice items, eliminate the answers you know are wrong. Then think about which of the remaining answers is correct.

Summarizing   Part B

On the lines below, write a summary of the third paragraph in the passage (9–14).

_____

_____

_____

_____

_____

_____

_____

_____

- To summarize a passage is to restate it in your own words.

- A summary should be much shorter than the original.

- A summary should not contain opinions.

Part C   Understanding Graphs and Other Visuals

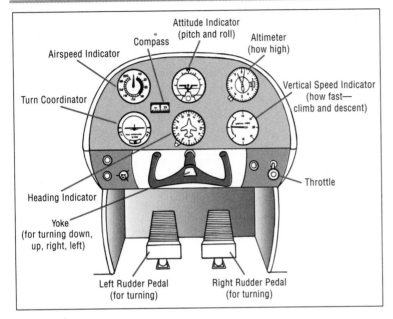

Diagrams

This diagram shows the instrument panel of a light airplane. The most important instruments have captions. Use the diagram and captions to answer the questions that follow.

1. What is the name for the "steering wheel" on the airplane?
   Ⓐ the altimeter
   Ⓑ the yoke
   Ⓒ the throttle
   Ⓓ the steering wheel

2. What is the name of the instrument that shows how high an airplane is?
   Ⓐ attitude indicator   Ⓒ airspeed indicator
   Ⓑ altimeter   Ⓓ heading indicator

3–4. Two instruments on this panel measure an airplane's speed. What are their names?

_____

Bar Graphs

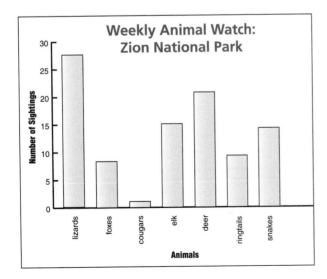

Read the bar graph. Then answer the questions.

5–6. Which animal was seen most frequently at the park?
_____ Which one was
seen least often? _____

7. How many foxes were seen?
   Ⓐ more than 30
   Ⓑ several hundred
   Ⓒ less than 15; about 13
   Ⓓ less than 10; about 9

8. You saw fifteen buzzards at the park. Add that information to the graph.

Symbols

The symbols in the chart to the left are used to convey information having to do with science and math. Use the symbols to complete the activity.

male	♂
female	♀
a second	I
a minute	II
greater than	>
less than	<

Replace each word in bold type with a symbol.

9. How many **male** babies and **female** babies are born every minute and every second? How many _____ babies and _____ babies are born every _____ and every _____?

10. Is the number of girls **greater than** or **less than** the number of boys? Is the number of girls _____ or _____ than the number of boys?

Thinking Critically About Science; Understanding Technical Terms

Part D

Read this passage. Think about whether you agree with what its author says.

Mars or Bust

Recently space scientists discovered that water exists on Mars. The existence of water means it is possible that life really does exist on "the red planet." The possibility of life on Mars means that we must waste no time in exploring our distant neighbor.

The discovery of life on Mars would be the single most important scientific event in history. Distant life forms may give us clues to our own past, or to the history of the earth. They may even allow us to glimpse what life forms of the future will be like.

Without doubt, the explorations of Mars would be costly. It may require billions of dollars. The cost is unimportant, however, compared to the benefits.

1. Do you think the author has done a good job of explaining why the exploration of Mars is a good idea? Why or why not? ___ yes ___ no

because: _____

_____

2. Which of the following objections to Mars exploration do you think the writer should have addressed?

Ⓐ Money would be better spent on solving problems here on earth.

Ⓑ Martians might not be very much fun.

Ⓒ Mars exploration is dangerous for space explorers.

Ⓓ Life on Mars might not be friendly, and it could even harm us.

3. Write your own opinion about this issue. Give at least two reasons why you think as you do.

_____

_____

_____

_____

_____

_____

Technical Terms and Root Words

| originate |
| transplant |
| polymer |
| microorganism |
| orbit |
| seismologist |

Write each word from the box to the left next to the correct root word

4. polus—"many" _____

5. orbis—"circle" _____

6. orig—"beginning" _____

7. seismos—"earthquake" _____

8. organism—"living thing" _____

9. trans—"across" _____

| nucleus (29) |
| digital (32) |
| seismograph (30) |
| reflective (32) |
| trough (33) |
| breaker (33) |

Write each word in the box to the left next to its meaning. Go back to the lesson shown in parentheses if you need to reread the word in context.

10. able to reflect light _____

11. lowest part between two waves _____

12. solid part of a comet _____

13. machine that records earthquakes _____

14. code made up of 0 and 1 _____

15. highest point of an ocean wave _____

Introduction

The famous writer Samuel Johnson described literature this way:

> ". . . a kind of intellectual light which, like the light of the sun,
> may sometimes enable us to see what we do not like."

Literature has many purposes:

- to make us think about important issues
- to entertain us
- to highlight conflicts people face as a part of life
- to teach lessons about how to behave
- to record the stories and legends of people around the world

Literature includes stories, poems, plays, fables, and many other kinds of writing. Chapter 6 will help you know how to read and think about literature. This, in turn, will help you enjoy a world rich in language and ideas.

Vocabulary for Literature

Literature has a language all its own. Knowing some of the words in this language will help you talk and write about literature in a thoughtful way. The words below form the beginning of a glossary of literary terms. You will learn new literary terms in each lesson in Chapter 6.

genre—type of literature, such as fiction, nonfiction, or mystery story

characters—the people in a story

narrator—the person who tells a story

point of view—how a narrator sees the events in a story: as an outside observer, or as a character who is part of the story

voice—the point of view from which a narrator tells a story:

- If a narrator uses the **first-person voice,** he or she is a character in the story and refers to himself or herself as **I.**
- If a narrator uses the **third-person voice,** he or she is an outside observer, and refers to all the characters as **he, she,** or **they.**

theme—the bigger, more important issue a work of literature addresses, such as love, loyalty, or hope

Previewing and Predicting

Think About Genre

When you preview literature, try to get a sense of what kind of writing you are about to read. Use what you know about genres to help you.

Read the genre descriptions below.

Genres
- **biography**—story of a real person's life, told by someone else
- **autobiography**—story of a real person's life, told by that person
- **fantasy story**—story that contains characters or events that can't possibly exist in real life, such as flying horses
- **realistic fiction**—story made up by an author which presents characters and events that could exist and seem real
- **fable**—very short tale, often with animals as characters, that teaches a lesson

Now write the name of each genre under the literature title that is most likely an example of it.

1. "The Wise Fox and the Foolish Coyote" _____

2. "My Life in the Movies" _____

3. "The Dragons of Dundee" _____

4. "The Life of Lotta Crabtree" _____

5. "Joshua Meets His Match" _____

Previewing Literature

When you preview, follow these steps:

- Read the title and decide what the genre of the story is.
- If you are reading a chapter book, read the information on the book cover. Also read the chapter titles.
- Read the first two or three paragraphs.
- Look at any pictures that accompany the story.

Making Predictions About Literature

When you make a prediction about a work of literature, use the genre to help you. For example, most biographies are written in time order—according to the sequence of events in the subject's life. If you come across a biography, you can guess that it will start by describing the subject's youth.

Practice Making Predictions

Preview the stories below.

	1	2

1
The Time Traveler
by Ernest Mayer

Jodi was well into the Sunday paper when something odd caught her eye. As she was flipping through the paper to find the comics, she happened to glance at the classified ads.

One job listing nearly leaped off the page. It said, "Wanted: Time Traveler." She read the ad with growing excitement. "No experience traveling through time required," it went on. "We train you."

Jodi copied down the phone number with trembling hands. "That job sounds perfect!" she said.

2
Time for Change
by Sandra Chu

Cam slammed the phone down in disgust. "That's the third rejection this week," he complained to his brother Nick. "What's a guy supposed to do to get a job around here?"

Nick shrugged. "It might help if you wore something besides those old jeans to your interviews," he said. "And you were late for the last one, weren't you?"

Cam didn't answer. Who did Nick think he was, bossing him around? Nick already had a job. He'd forgotten how hard it was to find one.

Now make some predictions about the stories. For questions 6–8, write Story 1 or Story 2 on the line.

6. Which story will probably be a fantasy? _____

7. Which story will probably have a serious **tone,** or feeling? _____

8. In which story will the character probably undergo a change in attitude? _____

9. How would you describe Jodi in Story 1? Fill in two circles.

  Ⓐ adventurous   Ⓒ fun-loving

  Ⓑ resentful   Ⓓ angry

10. How would you describe Cam in Story 2? Fill in two circles.

  Ⓐ angry   Ⓒ defensive

  Ⓑ fun-loving   Ⓓ honest

LESSON 36   Strategies for Fiction

VOCABULARY FOR FICTION

These terms are important to know when you talk or write about fiction stories.

main character
the most important person in a story

conflict
the main trouble or challenge faced by the main character

plot
the series of events that take place in a story; these events often involve a **problem** and a **resolution**

setting
the time and place in which a story happens

dialogue
the words characters say to each other; dialogue appears in quotes

Preview Realistic Fiction

The story you will read on the next few pages is a work of realistic fiction. To preview it, read the title on page 123. Then read the first three paragraphs of the story. After you have previewed it, answer these questions.

1. Who does the main character in the story seem to be?

   Ⓐ Lemon Brown   Ⓒ Greg Ridley

   Ⓑ Greg's dad   Ⓓ the narrator

2. How does Greg Ridley feel as the story begins?

   Ⓐ happy   Ⓒ sad

   Ⓑ angry   Ⓓ lonely

3. What is the setting of the story?

   _____

4. What conflict does Greg feel as the story begins? Finish this sentence.

   Greg wants to _____,

   but _____.

5. Do you think Greg will go home now, even though he expects a lecture? Why or why not?

   _____

   _____

   _____

Read the Story

Read the first part of the story to check your predictions. Stop when you see Think About It and then answer the questions.

The Treasure of Lemon Brown

by Walter Dean Myers

The dark sky, filled with angry, swirling clouds, reflected Greg Ridley's mood as he sat on the stoop of his building. His father's voice came to him again, first reading the letter the principal had sent to the house, then lecturing endlessly about his poor efforts in math.

"I had to leave school when I was thirteen," his father had said. "That's a year younger than you are now. If I'd had half the chances that you have, I'd..."

Greg had sat in the small, pale green kitchen listening, knowing the lecture would end with his father saying he couldn't play ball with the Scorpions. He had asked his father the week before, and his father had said it depended on his next report card. It wasn't often the Scorpions took on new players, especially 14-year-olds, and this was a chance of a lifetime for Greg. He hadn't been allowed to play high school ball, which he had really wanted to do, but playing for the community center team was the next best thing. Report cards were due in a week, and Greg had been hoping for the best. But the principal had ended the suspense early when she sent that letter saying Greg would probably fail math if he didn't spend more time studying.

"And you want to play *basketball*?" His father's brows knitted over deep brown eyes. "That must be some kind of joke. Now you just get into your room and hit those books."

That had been two nights before. His father's words, like the distant thunder that now echoed through the streets of Harlem, still rumbled softly in his ears.

It was beginning to cool. Gusts of wind made bits of paper dance between the parked cars. There was a flash of nearby lightning, and soon large drops of rain splashed onto his jeans. He stood to go upstairs, thought of the lecture that probably awaited him if he did anything except shut himself in his room with his math book, and started walking down the street instead. Down the block there was an old tenement that had been abandoned for some months. Some of the guys had held an impromptu checker tournament there the week before, and Greg had noticed that the door, once boarded over, had been slightly ajar.

Pulling his collar up as high as he could, he checked for traffic and made a dash across the street. He reached the house just as another flash of lightning changed the night to day for an instant, then returned the graffiti-scarred building to the grim shadows. He vaulted over the outer stairs and pushed tentatively on the door. It was open, and he let himself in.

The inside of the building was dark except for the dim light that filtered through the dirty windows from the street lamps. There was a room a few feet from the door, and from where he stood at the entrance, Greg could see a squarish patch of light on the floor. He entered the room, frowning at the musty smell. It was a large room that might have been someone's parlor at one time. Squinting, Greg could see an old table on its side against one wall, what looked like a pile of rags or a torn mattress in the corner, and a couch, with one side broken, in front of the window.

He went to the couch. The side that wasn't broken was comfortable enough, though a little creaky. From this spot he could see the blinking neon sign over the bodega on the corner. He sat awhile, watching the sign blink first green, then red, allowing his mind to drift to the Scorpions, then to his father. His father had been a postal worker for all Greg's life and was proud of it, often telling Greg how hard he had worked to pass the test. Greg had heard the story too many times to be interested now.

For a moment Greg thought he heard something that sounded like a scraping against the wall. He listened carefully, but it was gone.

Outside, the wind had picked up, sending the rain against the window with a force that shook the glass in its frame. A car passed, its tires hissing over the wet street and its red taillights glowing in the darkness.

Greg thought he heard the noise again. His stomach tightened as he held himself still and listened intently. There weren't any more scraping noises, but he was sure he had heard something in the darkness—something breathing!

He tried to figure out just where the breathing was coming from; he knew it was in the room with him. Slowly he stood, tensing. As he turned, a flash of lightning lit up the room, frightening him with its sudden brilliance. He saw nothing, just the overturned table, the pile of rags, and an old newspaper on the floor. Could he have been imagining the sounds? He continued listening but heard nothing and thought that it might have just been rats. Still, he thought, as soon as the rain let up he would leave. He went to the window and was about to look out when he heard a voice behind him.

"Don't try nothin' 'cause I got a razor here sharp enough to cut a week into nine days!"

❖　❖　❖　❖

Greg, except for an involuntary tremor in his knees, stood stock-still. The voice was high and brittle, like dry twigs being broken, surely not one he had ever heard before. There was a shuffling sound as the person who had been speaking moved a step closer. Greg turned, holding his breath, his eyes straining to see in the dark room.

The upper part of the figure before him was still in darkness. The lower half was in the dim rectangle of light that fell unevenly from the window. There were two feet, in cracked, dirty shoes from which rose legs that were wrapped in rags.

"Who are you?" Greg hardly recognized his own voice.

"I'm Lemon Brown," came the answer. "Who're you?"

"Greg Ridley."

"What you doing here?" The figure shuffled forward again, and Greg took a small step backward.

"It's raining," Greg said.

"I can see that," the figure said.

The person who called himself Lemon Brown peered forward, and Greg could see him clearly. He was an old man. His black, heavily wrinkled face was surrounded by a halo of crinkly white hair and whiskers that seemed to separate his head from the layers of dirty coats piled on his smallish frame. His

THINK ABOUT IT

Did Greg go straight home? ___ yes ___ no

What did Greg do? Why?

_____

_____

_____

_____

Greg hears a voice in the darkness. Who do you think it is?

_____

_____

_____

Now read on to see if your prediction is right.

pants were bagged to the knee, where they were met with rags that went down to the old shoes. The rags were held on with strings, and there was a rope around his middle. Greg relaxed. He had seen the man before, picking through the trash on the corner and pulling clothes out of a Salvation Army box. There was no sign of the razor that could "cut a week into nine days."

"What are you doing here?" Greg asked.

"This is where I'm staying," Lemon Brown said. "What you here for?"

"Told you it was raining out," Greg said, leaning against the back of the couch until he felt it give slightly.

"Ain't you got no home?"

"I got a home," Greg answered.

"You ain't one of them bad boys looking for my treasure, is you?" Lemon Brown cocked his head to one side and squinted one eye. "Because I told you I got me a razor."

"I'm not looking for your treasure," Greg answered, smiling. "*If* you have one."

"What you mean, *if* I have one," Lemon Brown said. "Every man got a treasure. You don't know that, you must be a fool!"

"Sure," Greg said as he sat on the sofa and put one leg over the back. "What do you have, gold coins?"

"Don't worry none about what I got," Lemon Brown said. "You know who I am?"

"You told me your name was orange or lemon or something like that."

"Lemon Brown," the old man said, pulling back his shoulders as he did so. "They used to call me Sweet Lemon Brown."

"Sweet Lemon?" Greg asked.

"Yessir. Sweet Lemon Brown. They used to say I sung the blues so sweet that if I sang at a funeral, the dead would commence to rocking with the beat. Used to travel all over Mississippi and as far as Monroe, Louisiana, and east on over to Macon, Georgia. You mean you ain't never heard of Sweet Lemon Brown?"

"Afraid not," Greg said. "What...what happened to you?"

"Hard times, boy. Hard times always after a poor man. One day I got tired, sat down to rest a spell, and felt a tap on my shoulder. Hard times caught up with me."

"Sorry about that."

"What you doing here? How come you didn't go on home when the rain come? Rain don't bother you young folks none."

"Just didn't." Greg looked away.

"I used to have a knotty-headed boy just like you." Lemon Brown had half walked, half shuffled back to the corner and sat down against the wall. "Had them big eyes like you got. I used to call them moon eyes. Look into them moon eyes and see anything you want."

"How come you gave up singing the blues?" Greg asked.

"Didn't give it up," Lemon Brown said. "You don't give up the blues; they give you up. After a while you do good for yourself, and it ain't nothing but foolishness singing about how hard you got it. Ain't that right?"

"I guess so."

"What's that noise?" Lemon Brown asked, suddenly sitting upright.

The story goes on to explain that the noise is caused by intruders, who the intruders are, and how Lemon Brown handles them. It also goes on to explain the "treasure" Lemon Brown so proudly speaks of. To finish this story, look for the works of author Walter Dean Myers in your local library.

Think About Literature

Reread the first sentence of the story on page 123.

6. What does the author compare the stormy sky to?

 Ⓐ Greg's mood   Ⓒ a treasure

 Ⓑ a hurricane   Ⓓ Lemon Brown

7. How does the storm add to the mood of the story?

 Ⓐ It makes the inside of the building seem cozy.

 Ⓑ It makes Greg seem smart for seeking shelter.

 Ⓒ It makes Lemon Brown seem cheerful by comparison.

 Ⓓ It makes the mood seem gloomy and depressing.

Reread these lines from the story:

"The upper part of the figure before him was still in darkness. The lower half was in the dim rectangle of light that fell unevenly from the window. There were two feet, in cracked, dirty shoes from which rose legs that were wrapped in rags."

8. What do the details help you predict about Lemon Brown?

 Ⓐ He is probably lost and scared.

 Ⓑ He is probably poor and homeless.

 Ⓒ He is an old friend of Greg's.

 Ⓓ He is probably dangerous.

9. How would you describe Greg's attitude toward Lemon Brown?

 Ⓐ He is afraid of Lemon—too afraid to think.

 Ⓑ He is unfriendly and even hostile.

 Ⓒ He trusts Lemon from the time he first sees him.

 Ⓓ He is friendly and seems interested in Lemon.

10. What did Lemon Brown have once, that he has now lost? Fill in two circles.

Ⓐ an ability to sing the blues   Ⓒ his ability to see clearly

Ⓑ his health   Ⓓ a family

11. What do you think Lemon Brown means when he says, "You don't give up the blues; they give you up"?

_____

_____

_____

12. Lemon Brown says, "You ain't one of them bad boys looking for my treasure, is you?" Also, he suddenly sits upright when he hears a noise. What do these details help you figure out?

Ⓐ Lemon Brown misses his wife and son.

Ⓑ Lemon Brown has probably had some bad experiences with the local kids.

Ⓒ Lemon Brown has worked things out with the local kids.

Ⓓ Lemon Brown is afraid of everything and everyone.

13. What do you think Lemon Brown's "treasure" is?

Ⓐ a stash of cash no one has found

Ⓑ something he loves dearly, from his past

Ⓒ a razor that can cut a week into nine days

Ⓓ a map that leads to a treasure

Understanding Dialect

Authors sometimes write dialogue the way their characters really speak. This is called using **dialect**. Authors have characters speak in dialect to make them seem authentic, or real.

14. Read these lines of dialogue. Fill in the circle that is an example of dialect.

Ⓐ "I'm not looking for your treasure."

Ⓑ "Rain don't bother you young folk none."

15. Most of Lemon Brown's dialogue is written in dialect, but only some of Greg Ridley's is. Why do you think the author chose to treat these characters and their speech differently?

_____

_____

16. Find an example of something Greg says that is spoken the way a real person might say it. Write it here.

_____

_____

Understanding Flashback

A **flashback** is a sudden shift in time, from the present to the past. In a flashback, a character remembers something that happened earlier.

17. Reread the first five paragraphs of the story on page 123. Put an X by the place where Greg's flashback begins.

18. Circle the sentence that tells you how long ago the lecture in the kitchen took place.

19. Write a number from 1–4 on the lines to show the order of these story events. Reread the first five paragraphs, if you need to.

____ Greg asks his father if he can play ball with the Scorpions.

____ Greg sits on the stoop of his building.

____ Greg's father lectures him.

____ The principal sends a letter home.

Making a Personal Response

There is no right or wrong answer to many questions having to do with literature. One such question is: **Did you like the story** as far as you read?

20. On the lines below, give your personal response to "The Treasure of Lemon Brown." Give at least one reason why you did or didn't like the story.

_____

_____

_____

_____

_____

LESSON 37   Strategies for Poetry

What Is Poetry?

Poetry is a special kind of writing that communicates a powerful feeling, idea, or picture using a few well-chosen words. The poet William Wordsworth began his famous poem "Daffodils" this way:

"I wandered lonely as a cloud."

This beautiful line gives a powerful picture—but the picture is a little different for every person. What does this line make you think of?

mental picture: _____

feeling: _____

About Poetry

- Poetry has its own form on a printed page—poetry **looks different** from ordinary text.
- A poem can be long or short. Some poems have a regular pattern of **rhyme** and **rhythm**, and others don't.
- Poets often use words in new, unusual ways.
- Only part of what a poem means is determined by the poet. Readers construct the rest of the meaning when they think about a poem.

Vocabulary for Poetry

These words are important when you read, think, and talk about poetry.

- **alliteration** repetition of sounds, especially consonant sounds
- **image** a mental picture created by the poet's words
- **metaphor** a comparison made by talking about one thing as if it were something else
- **simile** a comparison of unlike things, using the word like or as
- **symbol** something that stands for something else
- **tone** the overall mood or feeling of a written work
- **stanza** the lines that make up a unit within a poem, organized in a pattern that repeats
- **verse** lines of a poem with a loose pattern or no pattern

Metaphor is related to the word **metamorphosis,** which means "a change from one form to another." Both words come from the Greek root **meta,** which means "change." When writers use metaphors, they change our way of looking at something by comparing it to something completely different.

Read a Poem

Read the following poem. Think about the two things the poet is comparing.

Metaphor

by Eve Merriam

Morning is
a new sheet of paper
for you to write on.

Whatever you want to say,
all day,
until night
folds it up
and files it away.

The bright words and the dark words
are gone
until dawn
and a new day
to write on.

Think About Meaning

1. What two things is the poet comparing? Fill in the correct circle.

   Ⓐ words and paper

   Ⓑ writing about day and writing about night

   Ⓒ a new day and a blank sheet of paper

   Ⓓ bright words and dark words

2. What message does the poet seem to be giving?

   Ⓐ There is never enough time to say what you want.

   Ⓑ Day is more fun than night.

   Ⓒ If you don't finish a paper one day, finish it the next day.

   Ⓓ Every new day is a new beginning.

Listen to Sounds

3. Reread the poem and listen to the last word in each line. Underline the three words that rhyme in the second verse. Write the rhyming words here.

_____

4. Underline the three words that rhyme in the third verse. Write the rhyming words here.

_____ _____ _____

5. What is the theme of this poem?

Ⓐ friendship   Ⓒ loneliness

Ⓑ hope   Ⓓ nature

Extended Metaphor

Eve Merriam's poem on page 130 is called an **extended metaphor**. In this kind of poem a poet talks about one thing as if it were another for the entire length of the poem.

Think about the idea of extended metaphor as you reread the poem. On the lines below, write words or phrases that make you think of a new day or a blank sheet of paper.

	A new day	**a blank sheet of paper**
6. Stanza 1	_____	_____
	_____	_____
	_____	_____
7. Stanza 2	_____	_____
	_____	_____
	_____	_____
8. Stanza 3	_____	_____
	_____	_____
	_____	_____

Read Another Poem

Read this poem by William Wordsworth. Then answer the questions.

The Violet

by William Wordsworth

A violet by a mossy stone,

Half hidden from the eye,

Fair as a star, when only one

Is shining in the sky.

9. Which lines rhyme in the poem?

Ⓐ the first and second

Ⓒ the third and fourth

Ⓑ the second and fourth

Ⓓ the first and last

10. What is the poem mostly about?

Ⓐ a mossy stone

Ⓒ what is hidden from the eye

Ⓑ a star in the sky

Ⓓ a flower called a violet

11. In this context, **fair** (line 3) means "lovely." What two things is the poet comparing in lines 3 and 4?

Ⓐ a stone's shape and a flower's shape

Ⓑ the sky and the earth

Ⓒ a dark, fair sky and a violet, cloudy sky

Ⓓ a violet's beauty and the beauty of a star

12. What do you think the poet thinks and feels when he sees a violet?

_____

_____

_____

13. What do you think the theme of the poem is?

Ⓐ love

Ⓒ hope

Ⓑ beauty

Ⓓ loneliness

14. Restate the poem's message, or theme, in your own words.

_____

_____

_____

LESSON 38   Strategies for Plays

What Is a Play?

A play is a story that has been written for actors and actresses to perform on stage. The words below have to do with performing plays.

How a Stage Is Set Up

This diagram shows the main parts of a stage. Actors need to know the parts of a stage to follow the stage directions. Knowing how a stage is set up also will help you picture the play's action.

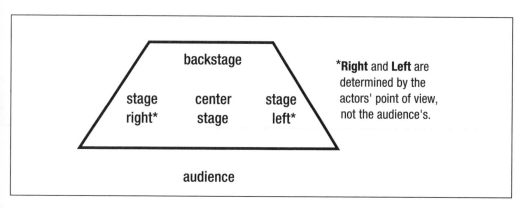

Preview a Play

The play you are about to read is based on a fable. Read the title on page 134. Read the cast of characters, the description of the setting, and the first few lines, through Hap's third set of dialogue. Then answer these questions.

1. Who do you think the main character in the play is? _____

2. What is the setting of the play? _____

3. What is King Zeke's problem at the beginning of the play?

   _____

4. What do you think King Zeke and Hap might do to solve this problem? _____

VOCABULARY
FOR PLAYS

cast of characters
the people in a play

scene
part of a play; where the action takes place in one stage setting

stage directions
directions that tell the actors how to move on stage and how to speak, usually in parentheses and italic type

disguise
what a character wears so that others will not recognize him or her

soliloquy
an actor talking to himself or herself, as if thinking aloud

aside
something a character says so the audience can hear, but the other characters cannot

Read a Play

Now read the play and check your prediction.

The Two Lions and the Wise Fox

Cast of Characters:

King Zeke, a tired old lion	Goat
Hap, a young, lazy lion	Two Rabbits
Calf	Donkey
Sheep	Fox

Setting: A lion's cave in the forest. A throne sits in the back of the cave, center stage. Near it is a huge rock. The entrance of the cave is stage left. Opposite, stage right, is another chair with a stool in front of it.

Scene 1: *(ZEKE stands alone in his cave. His crown is tilted, and he looks sad.)*

Zeke: *(Soliloquy.)* How sad I am! I can no longer hunt as I once did. Without food, I must die here in my cave.

(HAP enters stage left. He is wearing a hat with a feather in it.)

Hap: King Zeke, how are you? *(He bows, sits down on a chair, and puts his feet up on a stool.)*

Zeke: Not at all well. *(He sits down on his throne and sadly shakes his head.)* I am too old to hunt. I may as well lie down and die.

Hap: That's no way for a lion like yourself to talk! Don't be so gloomy. Let's put our brains together and think of a plan.

Zeke: It's no use. *(Sadly.)*

Hap: Hmmm. *(Deep in thought.)* You are old and tired and cannot hunt. I am young and lazy and hate to hunt. What can we do? *(He sits up suddenly.)* I have it!

Zeke: *(He perks up a bit.)* Yes?

Hap: I will let all the animals of the forest know that you are not well. Then I'll invite them to visit you here in the cave to say a last goodbye. Once the dumb critters are in here, **voila**[1]! Instant dinner!

Zeke: But when they see you, they will run in fear.

Hap: I will disguise myself as one of them. I'll be...I'll be a deer! Nothing could be easier.

Zeke: A very clever plan, indeed! Let's begin. I grow hungry.

Scene 2: *(ZEKE sits on his throne. HAP stands stage right disguised as a deer. He is crying into a handkerchief. CALF slowly enters the cave. She looks unsure about whether or not she should enter the cave. ZEKE greets her in a friendly way.)*

Calf: Greetings, King Zeke. *(She looks at HAP crying.)*

Zeke: Why hello, there, Calf! Do come in. I am very ill and will not be long in this world. Maybe you can cheer me up.

[1] **voila**! A French word meaning "There it is!" or "There you have it!"

READING TIP

Scene 2 tells you that this is a new part of the play. Ask yourself: What has changed since Scene 1? Form a mental picture of the new scene.

Hap: Oh, your majesty! We will all miss you so. *(He weeps louder.)*

(CALF walks closer. Suddenly Hap jumps and grabs CALF. He pulls CALF behind the rock. Just then SHEEP and GOAT approach the cave.)

Sheep: Hello, King Zeke. Are you home? *(SHEEP walks into the cave, followed by GOAT.)* I heard that you are not well, so I wanted to pay my respects. I brought my friend, Goat.

Zeke: Come in. Come in! Sheep and Goat, two of my favorite foods! I mean friends.

(As SHEEP and GOAT approach the throne, HAP jumps on SHEEP. ZEKE grabs GOAT. Both animals are pulled offstage. Shortly afterwards, a DONKEY and a pair of RABBITS visit and meet the same fate.)

    Scene 3: *(ZEKE and HAP are lying back in their chairs and patting their stomachs.)*

Zeke: I can't remember when I have eaten so well! Your plan was a fine one, indeed. We haven't had a visit yet from Fox. I wonder where he is.

(FOX walks up to the entrance to the cave.)

Fox: Hello, there! *(He calls into the cave.)* I hope that you are feeling better, King Zeke!

Hap: *(Aside.)* How lucky. Just in time for dessert!

Zeke: *(He calls out to FOX.)* I am still feeling very badly. But your visit will cheer me up. Come inside so I can see you.

Fox: If it's all the same to you, I'll stay right here.

Zeke: Why so shy? All of your friends came to visit me.

Fox: Yes, I know. It's very odd, though. I see their footprints going into the cave, but I don't see any footprints coming out. That's why I prefer to stay right where I am. I can wish you good health—and keep my own health, too!

The End

Think About the Play

5. The **moral** of a story is the lesson it teaches. What do you think the moral of "The Two Lions and the Wise Fox" is?

   Ⓐ Slow and steady wins the race.

   Ⓑ Cleverness is for today; wisdom is for tomorrow.

   Ⓒ Don't put off until tomorrow what you can do today.

   Ⓓ If at first you don't succeed, try again.

6. In a play, the action is moved forward by the dialogue. At the end of Scene 1, King Zeke says, "Let's begin. I grow hungry." What action takes place after he speaks these lines and before Scene 2 begins?

 Ⓐ Fox guesses that the deer is really a lion in disguise.

 Ⓑ The creatures visit King Zeke, one by one, in his cave.

 Ⓒ Hap disguises himself and tells the other creatures to visit King Zeke.

 Ⓓ Two rabbits get an unpleasant surprise.

7. In Scene 3, Hap says, "How lucky. Just in time for dessert." Who is he speaking to? (**Hint:** This dialogue is an **aside**. Reread the definition of **aside** on page 133.)

 Ⓐ all the characters   Ⓒ King Zeke

 Ⓑ Fox   Ⓓ the audience

8. Imagine that King Zeke gives another short soliloquy at the end of the play. What do you think he might say? Write your ideas here.

Zeke: *(Soliloquy)*_____

_____

_____

_____

9. Do you think the lion's plan will continue to work? Why or why not?

_____

_____

Rewrite a Story as a Play

On another sheet of paper, rewrite a short scene from a fiction story as a scene from a play. You could rewrite a scene from "The Treasure of Lemon Brown," or a scene from another story you've read.

LESSON 39   More Literary Terms

Old Terms, New Terms

You have learned these terms.

characters	main character	plot
metaphor	simile	dialect
theme	conflict	symbol

Here are some new terms and their meanings.

minor character—a less important character

protagonist—another word for the main character; also a word for "the good guy"

antagonist—person who challenges the main character; also known as "the bad guy"

cliché—overused phrase everyone is tired of

abstract—refers to an idea such as **wisdom** or **hope** that can't be understood through the five senses

concrete—opposite of **abstract**

allusion—an unexplained reference to a character, place, or work of literature, which the writer assumes the reader will know

SPELLING BUILDER

The words **allusion** and **illusion** are easily confused because they look and sound alike. An **illusion** is something that seems real, but isn't. An **allusion** is a reference to something else. When you use these words in your writing, check the dictionary to make sure you are using the right spelling and meaning.

Use Literary Terms

Write each literary term in the puzzle where it belongs.

Down

1. hero
2. opponent of the hero
3. unoriginal phrase

Across

4. reference to another work
5. can be touched, tasted, or smelled
6. opposite of **concrete**

Thinking Critically About Literature

Open to Interpretation

Literature is open to interpretation. To **interpret** something means to think about it in your own way, and come up with your own special view of it. Each time you read a story, poem, play, or other literary work, ask questions like these:

- What is the theme of this work? Does that theme have meaning for me?
- Do I see something in the work that other readers do not see? If so, what is it?
- Do I agree with what other people say about the work and its meaning? (If the answer is **no,** that's OK!)

Your Judgment Matters

You think critically about writing in science and social studies, and you can think critically about works of literature, too. These questions will help you make thoughtful judgments about what you like and don't like in the world of literature:

For Stories
- Did the author do a good job of making the characters seem real?
- Was the plot interesting and fun to follow?
- Did the writer choose words carefully, or does the story contain many clichés?
- Was the protagonist a strong character whom I liked and rooted for?

For Poems
- What is the poem trying to say?
- Did the poet do a good job of creating powerful images?
- Did the theme of the poem make sense? Do I agree with the message?
- If the poet used metaphors or similes, were they effective? Did they work for me?
- Did the poem make me feel a strong emotion or think deeply, or did it leave me cold?

Evaluate a Story

On the lines on page 139, write an evaluation of a fiction story and a poem. Try to answer some of the questions on page 138. Use as many literary words as you can. Some words have been suggested in the boxes.

characters	setting	plot	action
point of view	narrator	protagonist	

Story Title: _____

Author: _____

My Interpretation: _____

_____

_____

My Evaluation: _____

_____

_____

_____

_____

_____

Evaluate a Poem

verse	stanza	image	rhyme
metaphor	simile	voice	theme

Poem Title: _____

Poet: _____

My Interpretation: _____

_____

_____

My Evaluation: _____

_____

_____

_____

_____

_____

Part A

Previewing and Predicting; Thinking About Genre

Read the story titles below. Next to each one, write the genre that story is most likely an example of.

realistic fiction	fantasy	biography
	folktale	autobiography

1. "Ben Franklin's Life and Work" by Barnaby Zotes _____

2. "Those Rumors About Carla" by Maria Hernandez _____

3. "How I Became an Astronaut" by Melinda Perry _____

4. "The Crow and the Pitcher" _____

5. "Return of the Gravity Thieves" by Dan Diggs _____

Read each story beginning below. Then make predictions about what the stories will probably be like.

Story #1	Story #2
The Sly Bat and the Wise Squirrel	**Escape of the Vampire Bats**
One evening Bat woke up with a huge hunger. "How many insects will I need to catch to stop this awful grumbling in my stomach?" he groaned. The very thought of swooping through the dusky air catching bugs made him dizzy. "I will get Squirrel to help me catch bugs," Bat told his wife.	Count Borba awoke one chilly morning to a discovery that horrified him. The door to the dungeon had been left open! His worst fears were confirmed when he peered into the dungeon's dark depths. Every one of his trained fire-breathing bats was gone!
"Squirrel won't help," she said flatly. "You know that she despises you. Besides, Squirrel and her family are fast asleep."	"Pandora!" the Count shrieked. "Where is that vile chambermaid?" he yelled. It was the third time in a week she had forgotten to lock up some part of the castle at night.
"Not for long," said Bat with a grin.	

Write Story 1 or Story 2 to answer these questions.

6. Which story is probably a folktale? _____

7. Which story is probably a fantasy fiction story? _____

Mark one answer to each question.

8. The mood of Story #2 is _____.
   - Ⓐ happy and light-hearted
   - Ⓒ heart-warming
   - Ⓑ a little sad
   - Ⓓ spooky but silly

9. What will probably happen in Story #1?
   - Ⓐ Bat will learn a lesson.
   - Ⓒ Bat will solve a crime.
   - Ⓑ Squirrel will learn a lesson.
   - Ⓓ Squirrel will save thousands of lives.

10. What element in Story #2 could not possibly exist in real life?
    - Ⓐ fire-breathing bats
    - Ⓒ a person living in a castle
    - Ⓑ a man named Count Borba
    - Ⓓ a person forgetting to lock things three times in a week

11. Who do you think will outsmart who in Story #1?
    - Ⓐ Bat will outsmart the bugs.
    - Ⓒ Squirrel will outsmart her family.
    - Ⓑ Bat will outsmart his wife.
    - Ⓓ Squirrel will outsmart Bat.

Strategies for Reading Fiction and Plays

Part B

Write each term in the box next to its meaning.

main character	conflict	
setting	dialogue	plot

1. The words characters say to each other _____

2. Where and when a story takes place _____

3. The most important person in a story or play_____

4. The events that make up a story's action_____

5. The trouble or challenge the main character faces _____

Answer these questions using "The Treasure of Lemon Brown" on pages 123–126.

6. There are two settings in "The Treasure of Lemon Brown." What are they? Fill in one circle in each column.

at the beginning of the story

Ⓐ Greg's front steps

Ⓑ an abandoned building

Ⓒ Greg's back steps

Ⓓ Greg's kitchen

in the middle of the story

Ⓔ Greg's kitchen

Ⓕ a blues club

Ⓖ an abandoned building

Ⓗ a doctor's office

7. Which sentence best sums up the plot of the story?

Ⓐ Greg Ridley's poor math grades threaten his chances of playing basketball. When he seeks solitude in an abandoned building, he meets a poor old man whose wisdom might have something to offer him.

Ⓑ Lemon Brown lost his family and his ability to play the blues. While seeking shelter in an abandoned building, he meets a boy who can help him turn his luck around.

8. Find an example of *dialect* in the story. Write it here.

_____

_____

9. What themes does "The Treasure of Lemon Brown" seem to have?

Ⓐ nature, interdependence, cooperation

Ⓑ teamwork, sportsmanship, victory

Ⓒ peace, unity, togetherness

Ⓓ success, failure, loss

VOCABULARY FOR PLAYS

■ cast

■ stage

■ directions

■ soliloquy

■ scene

■ aside

■ audience

Write each word in the box to the left next to its meaning below.

10. where the action in a play takes place in one stage setting _____

11. the people in a play _____

12. words that tell actors how to move and speak onstage _____

13. words spoken that only the audience can hear _____

14. a speech that is meant to be thinking aloud _____

15. the people who watch a play _____

Answer these questions using "The Two Lions and the Wise Fox" on pages 134–135.

16. Where does **Scene 3** take place?_____

17. In **Scene 3,** when Fox calls into the cave, where is he standing on the stage?

    Ⓐ stage right   Ⓒ center stage

    Ⓑ stage left   Ⓓ backstage

TEST TIP

When answering test questions about a longer passage, look back at the passage for details. To answer question 17, reread the description of the **Setting** at the beginning of the play.

Strategies for Reading Poetry

Part C

Read the poem below. Then answer the questions.

"Dreams"

by Langston Hughes

Hold fast to dreams
For if dreams die
Life is a broken-winged bird
That cannot fly.

Hold fast to dreams
For when dreams go
Life is a barren field
Frozen with snow.

1. How many stanzas does the poem have?

   Ⓐ two   Ⓒ eight

   Ⓑ four   Ⓓ ten

2. Look for a metaphor in the first stanza. What is the poet comparing?

   Ⓐ a life without dreams and a bird with a broken wing

   Ⓑ a bird with a broken wing and a bird that can't fly

   Ⓒ a life with dreams and a life without them

   Ⓓ a dream and a bird

3. Look for a metaphor in the second stanza. What two things is the poet comparing?

   _____ and _____

4–7. Circle the rhyming words in the poem. Then write them here.

   Stanza 1: 4._____ and **5.**_____

   Stanza 2: 6._____ and **7.**_____

8. What is the theme of the poem?

    Ⓐ snow   Ⓒ birds

    Ⓑ life   Ⓓ dreams

9. What do you think the poet's message is?

_____

_____

10. The "broken-winged bird" is an image. What kind of mental picture does it give you?

_____

Part D   Thinking Critically About Literature

Think About Symbols

You have learned that a symbol is something that stands for an idea. Draw a line to match each symbol on the left with the idea it often stands for.

symbol	idea
1. fox	happiness
2. donkey	bravery
3. dove	cleverness
4. lion	gloom or confusion
5. darkness	peace
6. light	stubbornness

Think About a Poem

On the lines below, write your opinion of the poem "Dreams" by Langston Hughes.

7–9. My Interpretation (What I think it means): _____

_____

_____

10–12. My Evaluation (How good is it? Why?): _____

_____

_____

_____